The Big Walls

Monte Agnér North Face
Matterhorn North Face
Grandes Jorasses – Walker Spur
Eiger North Face
Aconcagua South Face
Nanga Parbat South Face
Dhaulagiri South Face

Kaye & Ward · London
Oxford University Press · New York

The Big Walls

HISTORY   ROUTES   EXPERIENCES

REINHOLD MESSNER

Translated by Audrey Salkeld

Matterhorn North Face, 1,100 m

Grandes Jorasses — Walker Spur, 1,200 m

◁ Eiger North Face, 1,800 m   Aconcagua South Face, 3,000 m

Nanga Parbat South Face, 4,500 m ▷

A Comparison

I am always being asked how the great walls of the Alps relate to those of the 8,000 metre peaks in the Himalaya; whether, for instance, you can compare the Eiger North Face with the Rupal Face of Nanga Parbat. The simple answer is — no, you can't. The pure mathematical ratio of Eigerwand : Rupal Face = 1 : 3 won't do. The Rupal Face, it is true, is three times as high as the Eigerwand but the comparison isn't as easy as that. The height above sea level, the different climate, susceptibility to storms — all are factors that must be taken into account besides sheer face height. The South Face of Aconcagua begins at a height where the Eigerwand leaves off, at around 4,000 metres. And if you are considering the South Face of Nanga Parbat, you must imagine a Matterhorn North Face on top of an Aconcagua South Face — that will give an idea of scale and steepness, but not of the higher altitude involved. It is simply not possible to draw this sort of comparison. A lot has been written about individual Big Walls, many photographs have been taken, but neither the literature nor the relative pictures can give a palpable overall impression of today's Big Wall Climbing. This is only possible from first-hand experience, although naturally it is expressed in first-hand accounts of this experience.

The South Face of Annapurna I (8,091 m) was the first wall of an eight-thousander to be climbed — in 1970 by a team under the leadership of Chris Bonington (G.B.). The route follows the left of the three pronounced spurs in the central section of the face.

The Big Walls

The concept of the 'Three Great Alpine Faces' evolved from the 'three last problems', and was expounded by Anderl Heckmair in his book, which has since become a classic.* The North Faces of the Matterhorn, the Grandes Jorasses and the Eiger characterise extreme Alpine climbing so exactly that until now they have represented the three shining goals, to which all true Alpinists aspired. Always there has been something of an aura about them — climbing them would guarantee a man recognition as a great mountaineer in the popular mind, even if technically he were not exceptional.

There are without doubt more difficult faces in the Alps, perhaps some that are even more beautiful, but these three remain indisputably the three greatest. The Northwest Face of the Civetta, the Laliderer Walls, the Frêney Spur on Mont Blanc, the North Face of the Droites, the Northeast Face of the Piz Badile, the West Face of the Dru — all these are big and extremely difficult, but they each lack some ingredient which prevents them from ranking alongside the Big Three.

Their worth, these three, apart from their historical importance, lies in my view in their particular combination of summit height, relatively great technical difficulty, their admixture of rock and ice climbing, and — not least — in the fact that none of them offers an easy way off once the route has been begun.

To project this idea of the Three Great Alpine Faces a stage further and nominate the Three Big Faces of the World, new criteria must be agreed, since following those that governed the Alpine selection, all the Big Walls of the Himalaya and Karakorum would qualify. The South Face of Annapurna, the West Buttress of Makalu — both these would be candidates along with the Rupal Flank on Nanga Parbat, the Southwest Face of Everest, and also — although these three are as yet unclimbed — the South Pillar of K2, the South Face of

* Die Drei Letzten Probleme der Alpen. Published by F. Bruckmann, Munich, 1949.

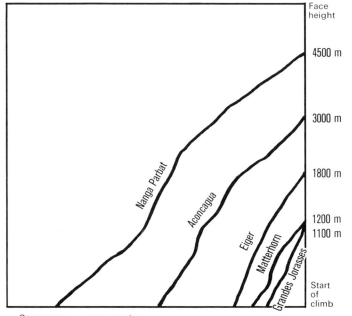

Steepness — cross section

'eight-thousanders', the world's highest mountains; the *South Face of Aconcagua* since this is the biggest wall in the Americas and also to be found on the highest peak in the Andes — moreover it is extremely difficult; and the *Eiger North Face* because it is the biggest sheer drop in the Alps, together with the fact that it is also one of the Three Great Alpine Faces. These are the Three Great Faces of the World.

At the current stage of mountaineering development when extreme climbers are looking beyond the Alps to remote areas further afield, the Big Walls of the World offer an exciting prospect. Yet though these include such three-star attractions as the Dych-Tau North Face in the Caucasus, the Troll Wall in Norway, the granite hulk of El Capitan in California, and the massive ice flanks of Mount Cook in New Zealand — to name but a few — the Rupal Wall, the South Face of Aconcagua and the Eigerwand still remain the three 'classical' objectives.

It is interesting to recall that during the first ascents of all five faces the climbers found themselves in life-or-death predicaments, facing borderline situations that in each case were unique in mountaineering history. And this notwithstanding that in each case, these were the best mountaineers of the particular epoch who were involved.

Today there must be several hundred climbers who have climbed all three big North Faces of the Alps, and to get to know them will continue to be an important ambition for a climber of stature, since any new terrain that still exists here can only be of second-rank. But on a world scale, things are different; the majority of Himalayan faces have yet to be climbed, and the question arises whether it is not more interesting to undertake a worthy virgin face than to repeat a 'classic'. Nevertheless, the time is dawning when a sporting mountaineer's life ambition might be to climb not just the three big faces of the Alps, but also those of the world.

Lhotse, and of course, the great southern ramparts of Dhaulagiri.

In the same way as for the Alps, the final selection included faces from three separate regions involving three different types of climbing (because of their different geological structure), so when selecting the Big Walls of the World, one takes first into account the highest and geographically most important mountain ranges of the world, and then the form of the faces in question, their background history and their climate. Maintaining the criteria of summit height, technical difficulty, isolation, and choosing from the highest faces of the mountain ranges of the various continents, there is no doubt what the eventual selection has to be:

The *Rupal Face on Nanga Parbat* because it is the biggest Big Wall in the world, and as such, obviously the highest face in the Himalayan region and Asia — at the same time, it is located on one of the fourteen

8

Last Problems

In the years following World War I, the first of the big and extremely difficult faces of the Alps were climbed. It is true that before then Preuss, Dulfer and Dibona had achieved an incredible standard of free-climbing, but this had, for the most part, taken place on relatively small Alpine faces. And although Dibona had made the first ascent of the huge southern side of Croz del Altissimo, he had failed on the North Face of the Furchetta, as did Hans Dulfer a short while later. And the Northwest Face of the Civetta, which Preuss so coveted, was too great a challenge for Alpinists at that time — too difficult, too large, too unpredictable. The East Face of the Monte Rosa and that of the Watzmann had been climbed in the second half of the 19th century; for sheer bulk they surpassed the biggest Dolomite climbs, but they lacked that extra technical

difficulty, that extra steepness that, for climbers, distinguishes a 'wall' from a 'flank', making it a worthy problem. This steepness and severity could be found in the great Dolomite walls that Emil Solleder was climbing in the mid-twenties, and about which he wrote in 'Die letzten grossen Wandprobleme in den Dolomiten' (Last Big Wall Problems in the Dolomites).

We know that later on far harder and more important routes were opened up in the Dolomites and that of course there still exist today climbing problems waiting to be solved there, but it was in the Western Alps that the so-called 'last problems' were sought. Besides pure rock climbing they offered the added challenge of passages of ice; they were also subject to more sudden storms and bivouacs were more frequent. From a climbing point of view, the big combined faces of the Alps were not technically harder than the Dolomite walls, but they were more massive and, because of the

10

◁ Cho Oyu (8,153 m) is relatively easily ascended from the North, but its southern flank is very steep. This face has not been attempted up till now, at least not seriously, although a logical possible route exists, following the curving spur in the central section of the face.

Everest (8,848 m) and Lhotse (8,511 m) lie so close together that it has long been questioned in geographical circles whether in fact the two summits should really be considered as separate eight-thousanders. In any event their southern aspects present separate problems.

ice and inclement weather, potentially more lethal. Sixteen years passed after the first of the big Dolomite walls was climbed (the North Face of Monte Agner), before the North Face of the Eiger received its first ascent in 1938, the most spectacular and notorious of the 'Three Last Problems'.

And another sixteen years were to pass before in 1954 a French expedition launched an attack on the 3,000 metre high South Face of Aconcagua. This represented a new phase in extreme climbing. Although the rock and ice problems were no less than those of the big Alpine walls, the face itself was twice the size. Moreover, the route rose to a height of almost 7,000 metres above sea level, a height at which the rarefied air presented a serious hazard.

After this 'last problem', it was difficult to foresee further advance, and yet, again another sixteen years later, in 1970 the Rupal Face of Nanga Parbat was climbed, the biggest of the mighty Himalayan faces. Again the difficulties were extreme, although not of the order of the Walker Spur. The route traced up this 4,500 metre rock and ice wall led to the summit of one of the fourteen 8,000 metre peaks, up to a height for which weeks of acclimatisation are required and which can only be withstood for very limited periods.

And so, with the climbing of this face, people are again looking around for 'last problems', but a significant advance is no longer possible. It took four mountain-climbing generations to make the step from the conquest of the North Face of Monte Agner, the highest of the Dolomite walls, to the first ascent of the Rupal Flank — fifty years of hard-won experience, commitment and sacrifice.

If it has been my good fortune to have succeeded in climbing these five great walls, it is only because I have approached them gingerly and taken my time. And if today I am in the position to review them objectively, this is because I can draw on my own experience, experience I have been privileged to gain.

The Watzmann East Face, first climbed in 1881 by Johann Geill, a Ramsau mountain guide and the Viennese, Otto Schück. This is not one of the Big Walls in Reinhold Messner's opinion despite its 2,000 metres face height, since its difficulties lie far below those of the Rupal Face of the Eigerwand.

Walls and Summits

Big Walls have fascinated me since childhood. Then everything was relative. When at the age of 16, with my young brother Günther, I climbed the North Face of the Sass Rigais in the Geislerspitzen near our home, I certainly knew about the Eiger North Face, but of Aconcagua's South Face and the Rupal Face, I had heard nothing. Therefore it was the Eigerwand that was the distant goal of my climbing ambition.

The reason we didn't go and attempt it that same summer was because our respect for such faces matched their reputation. At that time, too, I held all other climbers in great respect — if I invited one to do a route with me, I always climbed second on the rope. That way I learnt a lot. From Sepp Mayerl, whose job was roofing church towers in East Tyrol, I learnt how to organise belays; and thanks to Heini Holzer, a master chimney-sweep from South Tyrol, I lost the apprehension I felt at the prospect of extreme climbing.

I ceased seconding superior partners only when I found that things went faster if we exchanged leads. Later on, for safety reasons, I climbed almost exclusively alone. Now, if I share a rope with Heindl Messner or Peter Habeler, it makes no difference to me whether I or they climb in front. We can move fast and I have no qualms about safety. Alternating leads is the most natural way of climbing and provides the most variety. This is an especial advantage on the very Big Walls where the wellbeing and safety of the individual climber are prime considerations.

In the early days it was the difficulties of a route that were its main attraction for me; when I started climbing abroad, suddenly it was the summit that became more important. The summit, the point at which all aspiring lines come together, only reached after days — sometimes after long weeks — of effort,

12

this has about it something liberating, something conclusive for me . . . even though a descent has to follow a climb, and even though descent from a seven- or eight-thousander can be more dangerous than the ascent.

Every climber has to seek his own goals from his own point of view, and today in the atmosphere of mountaineering freedom that exists, nothing is taboo. I find the greatest personal satisfaction and the widest expression on high summits, summits reached by climbing hard Big Walls.

No record-breaking nor promise of glory fascinates me like the challenge of Possibility — a sporting pastime that people would once have called 'adventure'. It is not a thirst for danger, still less a gamble with death; it is the Step-into-the-Unknown, the construction of a link between the base of a mountain and its summit.

A Big Wall must not be embarked upon carelessly — experience, endurance, a conception of what it's all about, and above all, self-discipline — all these are necessary to overcome the crises that might be encountered.

Fun and reality, success and failure, life and death keep close company, as do heat and cold, sunshine and storm, rock and ice. It is not heroic to launch one-self into borderline-situations regardless of conse-quences. In mountaineering a hero does not live long; to know no fear can mean perhaps not coming back.

Only a man, a mortal man, with all his natural fears and weaknesses, his commonsense and his instinctive will to survive, can establish the respect necessary to climb these big faces and survive. Perhaps with his technological successes, man has lost something of his own measure, perhaps his relationship with the natural forces and with the world have become so distorted that only in a life-or-death situation can he rediscover himself.

Sometimes when I am climbing and all is going well, I make a decision whether to turn back or to go on, and it is all logical, problem-free and without

danger. It seems that nothing could go wrong and in any case I could quickly reverse the decision if necessary. And then perhaps, only a short while after, it suddenly becomes impossible to change one's mind. I feel then that there is only one solution, one way out, and each step I take is determined by the mountain or the natural forces and is heavy with fate.

To escape such a potentially dangerous situation, if it persists, is no simple matter. In legends of valour, the hero will pitch himself against Death and so overcome him. For my part, I have never knowingly sought to overpower death, never challenged it. In the face of prolonged danger, I have instinctively drawn into myself, submitted to it in the same way as one would accept ecstacy or terror.

Many such critical moments live in my memory, and as I write this book of the most outstanding of them, I can see again the clear starry sky over Mont Blanc as it was at the time of the bivouac on the Walker Spur. I can feel the soles of my boots slipping in the exit

K2 (8,611 m) on the left, and Broad Peak (8,047 m), the two big peaks in the Karakorum on which there are still many new routes waiting to be climbed. On K2 (also known as Chogori), for instance, several possibilities have caught the imagination of expedition mountaineers — its Southern Pillar, its West Ridge and its North Face.

cracks on the Eiger; the icy wind catches me in the face on the summit ridge of Aconcagua. Encircled by sky, I crouch on the summit slopes of the Matterhorn North Face whilst a loose snow-slide pours over me. For days I stumble alone down the Diamir Valley, completely exhausted and my brother lost.

There are tours and expeditions that run smoothly without a hitch and one relates them happily afterwards, but how easily and quickly they are forgotten. There are others of which it is hard to speak, but these I will never forget. They lie deeper and their pain and their shadow accompany me every day of my life.

Monte Agnér North Face

I have been climbing Big Walls for ten years, ten years during which I have made many other worthwhile mountain tours, and have continually been gaining new experience. I had of course not begun with Big Walls, but with small, with walking routes and easy climbing in the Dolomites around my home. And my later successes I attribute to those years — from the time I was five until my twentieth year — when I occupied myself with climbing on easy and moderately difficult terrain. From this experience I developed a certain instinct for mountain country that has stood me in good stead ever since and helped me over and again to make the right decision when confronted with a crisis situation that could so easily have proved fatal.

Growing up in the Dolomites, I first learned to climb on rock, and once I had completed many of the bigger Dolomite faces, I went on to attempt hard ice face climbs in my native South Tyrol, thus establishing a sound basic knowledge of both disciplines, rock and ice climbing, before going on to the Western Alps for the first time.

On top of that, several winter ascents gave me experience of climbing mixed routes in the worst imaginable conditions. This served to confirm me in my idea of just how much skill and practice, purpose and self-discipline are necessary to succeed on an 8,000 metre peak.

As an introduction to the Big Walls, therefore, I am including the story of the first winter ascent of the Agnér North Face, which at 1,500 metres is the biggest vertical face in the Dolomites. It was first climbed in 1921 by Franco Jori, Arturo Andreoletti and Antonio Zanutti, and even today is considered to be one of the most serious routes in the Eastern Alps. I offer it as an example of the type of climb that can afford the preparatory experience for the Big Walls.

In the Shadow of Monte Agnér

Snow. . .

brambles, trees, and rearing above them, the Agnér wall, dark above the Lucanotal, as we stamped our way to the foot of the climb. We were three — Heindl Messner, Sepp Mayerl and I, Sepp in the lead. Suddenly he stopped. 'A lot of powder snow on the ledges', he remarked drily. It was 29 January 1968.

It had snowed a few days before. Our eyes followed the line of chimneys on the North Face. We were looking for cracks and ledges. The storm had blown almost all the snow away from the northern edge and it looked much more inviting than the choked chimneys of the North Face. Cascades of ice and firmly-packed snow filled them. Thinking to myself that this would be a difficult winter route, I groped forward awkwardly a few steps more, my eyes still riveted to the Face. The weather looked as if it would hold, so I continued.

On some rocks just below the start, we took a short rest. The overall prospect still seemed good. We therefore discussed the most feasible way to tackle this 1,500 metre rock wall. In our minds we linked cracks, ribs and ledges together into a possible line — and it soon became apparent that it would be a very long one, too long perhaps for our courage. Would we be better to give up here and now? 'No — we should try it at least', Heindl encouraged. For the next few minutes we debated which way to tackle the first 200 metres; which of the two possible routes would offer the least resistance. The main chimney was overflowing with ice and snow, the system of cracks and slabs to the right of it were grey-white as if freshly sprinkled with sugar. We would have to leave the decision till we were there.

In the event it was made for us: when we reached the start we were confronted with fixed ropes! A team from Trieste had begun in the autumn to prepare the route for a winter ascent, so we learned later. We plumped now for the prepared route to the right of the main chimney and quickly gained height. About 100 metres up, the fixed ropes ended. We had been given a sheltered foretaste of things to come, but now we were on our own! All the cracks were iced up and everywhere was covered with new snow. It was not yet too steep and we were able to climb steadily at a good pace. Things went smoothly to the foot of the first flight of slabs, but suddenly it seemed as if all further progress was barred to us. I climbed a few metres higher and immediately retreated. Resignedly, I called back to my two companions who were belaying me from a gully, 'It's no good, it won't go. There's too much new snow!' But there were no obvious alternatives, so I tried again. I kept telling myself, it's just new snow, it will go with time and patience. And slowly I climbed higher. I chipped away with my hammer, fashioning little holds for my stiff fingers in the frozen mass.

After another 80 metres

the wall became so steep that under the circumstances we dared not contemplate climbing it free. We would have to peg it. Like a mighty paunch, the grey-yellow dolomite rock bellied out overhead. Seen from below, it was all foreshortened, but I knew there must still be another 1,000 metres separating us from the summit. Metre by metre we placed the pitons, dangling in our etriers. A 1,000 metres of artificial climbing, I thought, that was not my scene! Either we must continue by climbing it free, or we must turn back. This face was simply too big to climb in anything but classic style.

Everything around us was very steep and there was

Monte Agnér (2,872 m) in the Pala Group; its precipitous North Face is the biggest rock wall in the Dolomites. Reinhold Messner has been responsible for three 'firsts' on this mountain: first winter ascent of the Northern Ridge; a year later the first winter ascent of the North Face, and the first complete ascent of the Northeast Face.

already a breathtaking drop beneath us. But ever since we had been on this face, we had been out of touch with reality. The valley far below seemed quite remote, a different world. Up here, lost like wanderers in the wilderness, we were divorced from all beginning and all end. The world around, the valleys and the mountains, seemed as distant to me as the Universe from Earth. The only thing that now existed was the Agnér Wall.

From a picture we had with us, we tried to orientate ourselves. If we penduled to the left, we must surely come into the recess of the main chimney, and there it would not seem to be so steep. Photographs are essential to work out where one is on a giant face like this but a single shot can never capture the finer details. In the deep chimney we trampled out a little platform, sending showers of snow down into space. Above us balconies of snow, icicles and smooth walls. Rope's length by rope's length we struggled up. Slowly it began to get dark, and still no place for a bivouac. On top of that, the chimney was now quite vertical.

I would happily have given up the lead. When we started the climb I had taken on the responsibility for this first day, and now it would soon be night. We had to find somewhere for the night, and quickly!

I beavered away in the depths of the gully, hammering steps in the pressed snow, and at last managed to insert one sound piton, then I groped higher up the smooth chimney. I began to feel more secure. I had managed to shake off my anxiety and dejection. Inch by inch I climbed cautiously up. For my feet there was nothing but tiny, sloping holds; my hands I pressed flat against the opposing walls of the chimney. All the pitons left from summer ascents were now buried under layers of ice and snow, and there were scarcely any crevices at all into which a peg could be placed. At last, in a natural hole, I was able to insert one tiny, horizontal piton. That was all.

The first stars were already out. Press on! Time was running out. I climbed free on natural holds and steps, with legs and hands wedged either side of the chimney till it became too wide and I was unable to grope my way further upwards. What now? I balanced in the chimney and hammered tentatively at all the dents and cracks. No peg would hold. I glanced enquiringly down at my comrades who were standing 20 metres below, watching my every move. We didn't have any expansion bolts with us. My calf muscles were aching. Turn back? We had failed then? I summoned up my last ounce of strength.

In front of me the armour of the face was interrupted by a hole. A snow balustrade had built up on the lower lip of this hole. Was this the answer? Would it hold my weight? Quickly I knocked off the loose snow and wormed my fingers into the hard compact snow underneath. If it didn't hold my companions below would be buried and I, in all probability, would come off with it. But at that moment I feared a possible fall far less than the prospect of having to climb up again. 'Give me some slack!' I yelled, 'And watch out!' I hurled myself into the hole . . . and rolled down inside a roomy cave. I was safe. As I fumbled in the dark for two belay pegs, I speculated what might have happened if the snow balcony had given way.

Sepp and Heindl were amazed to see my legs vanish into the hole and then my head reappearing. At first they couldn't believe that we really had found a safe place for the night; then they too climbed up and satisfied themselves it was so. We would bivouac in this eagle's nest. It was obvious as soon as we were all in it together that it was too small. Too small to sit, to small to stand, too small to lie down – it was just big enough for us to crouch in. We sipped warm lemon juice and took stock of our position. According to the route description, the section we had just climbed was easy compared to the second half of the face. Obviously the 20-metre overhanging crack directly above our heads must be one of the key pitches to the whole climb. We had gained only 300 metres in height so far. It was too little. At this rate, it would take three or four days to reach the summit.

After a while

we packed ourselves into our cave like sardines in a tin. Any movement had to be announced in advance and effected conjointly. We dozed in snatches. In the same way as we had fortuitously discovered our eyrie the night before, so too the next morning, the way out was revealed.

A jammed block formed the roof of our cave.

Intermittently powder snow came down from somewhere above. A weak ray of light filtered through a loophole. Perhaps it led up to the main chimney? I investigated. After a good ten minutes I was out. A stroke of luck this hole, but damned narrow. 'We shouldn't have had breakfast till afterwards', I shouted down to Sepp and Heindl once I had eased myself through. After a difficult pitch in the chimney, it widened out a bit, but no sooner had I reached a level stance on the right hand wall, than the whole couloir began to creak and then to roar. Far above me a snow buttress had broken away. In a matter of moments it would carry me with it, I thought, and convulsively I grabbed hold of the peg. Everything became dark. I could feel something tugging at the rope. It must be the loose snow sweeping down. When I ventured to peep out, the chimney looked just as quiet and gloomy as it had before. Sepp and Heindl, secured to their separate stances, shouted excitedly. I looked like a snowman, completely white, covered in

Other mountaineers may prepare their proposed winter ascents with fixed ropes during the autumn, but Reinhold Messner prefers not to adopt these tactics. He climbed the Agnér North Face, therefore, with the minimum of equipment and applies the same 'fair means' principles to his Big Wall climbing.

The equipment of ten years ago was lightweight and good in comparison to that of the inter-war years, but against that of today, it was still quite primitive. Jammed nuts were unknown.

powder snow. I shook myself, hammered in a second peg, and down below they knew that everything was all right.

Sepp took over the lead. Following a crack system on the left side of the couloir, he climbed to the top of a spur, as indicated in the guidebook. From there a little sloping gully led up in to the middle section of the face.

The waiting at the belays

seemed to last longer and longer. We got very cold. Where was the sun? The shadow of Monte Agnér could be seen cast on the other side of the valley. Therefore it must be midday. Sepp struggled up an overhanging crack. His puffing and panting betrayed how difficult it was. We made very slow progress.

Silently, meanwhile, the shadow of Monte Agnér drew back. Heindl and I brought up the rear with the rucksacks. That made us warm, but all too soon we cooled off again. The shadows were lengthening noticeably. They already fell across the villages of Listolade and Taibon, which would soon disappear from view completely. We wondered how many more times we should experience it before the climb was through. Hour after hour we had seen the shadows cast by our mountain, but never once had the sun so much as touched upon the North Face. Soon after Sepp had found another cave for our second bivouac, a few rays of sun lit upon the North flank to our right. At one point only did they seem to reach the rocks; that was where we had bivouaced the winter before. We were not as high as that now.

Soon the sun had gone again, without reaching us. The night crept out of the valleys and swallowed everything. With the coming of darkness, something like lameness and depression seized me. I knew we should never escape the shadows for the entire length of our climb.

Heindl Messner, a distant relation of Reinhold Messner, an instructor with the Alpinschule Südtirol (Vilnöss, Dolomites), seen here in the exit pitches on Monte Agnér.

One by one the first stars twinkled over the summit; Sepp pulled out the cooker and its glow lit up our red down jackets. This second bivouac was roomier than the first. We lay, all three alongside each other, some 900 metres above the start of the climb.

The next morning the main difficulties would begin. We must get a good rest and recover our strength. My glance slid along the walls of the cave out to the starry sky. The final 600 metres floated before me in imagination: slabs, cracks, overhangs . . . ice and snow. Again no sunshine. Since we had left home we had lived only in shade or darkness. Whatever had made this winter ascent seem to me to be worth striving for? Sunshine? Daytime? Well it was certain that these only existed in my dreams.

Now it was night

and I was alone with the stars and two sleeping companions. We were still far from the top. None of us knew the way ahead. I even doubted whether there was a way ahead, whether perhaps insurmountable difficulties would yet confront us. Two days earlier we had started this climb in shadow; the sun rose, sank, rose again. But day for us meant only shadow; at night we had the stars. I gazed up at them strewn across the sky, haphazardly, disconnected; big and small, pallid and cold. In my mind I drew them together, concocting star pictures which I then let fall apart into a tangled swarm of bright points. Then I thought about how far away they were and I struck infinity. Finally I nodded off briefly.

Again I was awake. The stars shivered. A force for inactivity, that's what night was, a time when everything seemed gloomy and hopeless. The day before I had felt able to face anything and had been pleased at the prospect of the difficulties ahead. But at night, alone, I became a coward, even to myself.

The shadow of Monte Agnér

again fell behind us across the Lucano Valley. We had already climbed a few more pitches over rimy slabs to the left of the main chimney. The rocks here had been swept clean of snow by the storm and only in the cracks and hollows out of the wind were fine snow crystals poised. We had to move across eastwards to gain access to the upper third of the face. We had by this time reached a height level with the summit of the Spiz d'Agnér, the eastern neighbour of our mountain. Again and again I would compare our height with that of the Spiz. Two more rope's lengths. The Spiz d'Agnér is no dwarf on the summit crest of the Pale di San Sucano, but the Monte Agnér towers far above it. Its shadow projected across the Lucano Valley showed this clearly.

What a picture! The whole mountain group was thrown in perfect silhouette onto the other side of the valley: Torre Armena, Monte Agnér, Spiz d'Agnér. The individual shape of each peak was clearly visible. Only their colour was lost in the uniform greyness.

Above us rose a spur of rock, steep and impressive. We read the guidebook directions. 'Upwards on very steep slabs until forced back into the main chimney by the verticality.' This is where we were now. I traversed along a crest of snow to just beneath the chimney and immediately came back. It was no good. There was no going further by this route. The chimney was full of ice mushrooms.

The conditions of the original route forced us to opt for the vertical spur to the left of the chimney, as presenting the only possible way up. The wind had done some useful work on it.

I began to climb the first pitch of the spur; there were only the smallest of holds for hands and feet and the difficulty was Grade VI. A steep gully led upwards. Soon it became easier but then we met new problems. A shallow crack, choked with snow, had to be negotiated. Again the progress was interminably slow. The

shadows on the other side of the valley seemed to move forward more quickly, quietly and steadily. Now they broke up on the sharp edges of the Pale di San Lucano.

Our climbing tempo

became faster. I felt as if I had the strength to take on whatever faced us, and I pressed on, steadily gaining height. I was overcome with a feeling of lightness. Nothing could stop me now. I had the strongest conviction that we would succeed and was filled with happiness!

Already the shadow of our mountain had withdrawn wedge-shaped into the valley towards Torre Trieste. The sun must already, therefore, be quite low.

We were some 200 metres below the summit.

We would have liked to bivouac here but could find no suitable spot. There were still two hours before dark. That should be sufficient to bring us to the summit slopes! From the two alternative routes given in the guidebook, we chose the right hand one. A massive crack system — and then the summit couloir.

Without so much as using another peg, we literally raced up the next few pitches, four or five — perhaps more.

Just one last crumbling overhang—

'Shove in a peg!' I heard Sepp grumble below, and soon I was up, off the North Face, out of the shadows. I stood in the light of the setting sun. 'We're out!' I shouted, as if I couldn't believe it myself. The summit ridge seemed quite close. The sun shone upon it. But when Heindl and Sepp joined me, the sun had gone down. There remained only a red shimmer over the horizon.

Dimensions

If someone had said to me after that first winter ascent of the Agnér North Face, that this same Monte Agnér was only a klettergarten, a training ground, I would not have been merely astounded, I would have been incensed. Nowadays I realise that a peak like this compared to the great mountain faces of the world, does have the character of a klettergarten; and because of its relatively low height above sea level, it cannot be compared with a face like the Jorasses, let alone with Annapurna.

The relation in which one sees these faces, depends on one's individual viewpoint. Someone who climbs exclusively in the Wilder Kaiser would regard the Cima Grande as huge perhaps. Kasparek, in turn, looked upon the Cima Grande in winter as a training climb for the Eigerwand.

There are similar training grounds all over the Alps, and in Japan, California, South Africa, Norway and in the Tatra — anywhere in fact where there are climbers wishing to prepare themselves for the Big Walls.

Such klettergartens play an important role for the climbers resident in the vicinity, even if seen on a worldwide scale they have only secondary importance.

Recently I heard of a 17-year old who hiked to the Monte Agnér to solo the North Face. A few days later I met an 18-year old who in a single summer had climbed the Walker Spur, the Blaitière West Face, the North Faces of the Triolet and Courtes, the Cassin Ridge on the Torre Trieste as well as the Grosshorn North Face and a few others. The North Face of the Cima Grande he had already done — when he was fifteen.

These young climbers have not lost anything of that respect due to Big Walls — that is manifestly clear by the style in which they have executed their climbs — nor have they taken bigger risks; they have merely extended a few dimensions. And in the future when, building on the experience of earlier climbing generations, they search for bigger goals commensurate with their skills, it is on the Big Walls that they will find these goals.

Matterhorn North Face

Tho battle for the Matterhorn signalled the end of the Golden Age of Mountaineering when all the great Alpine peaks were conquered. The desire to be the first to stand upon its summit had eclipsed much of the romantic idealism that had characterised early Alpinism, and in addition the old superstitious fear of mountain spirits had disappeared. Rivalry was widespread amongst the leading mountaineers of the day. It was for this reason that 'the most beautiful Alpine peak' came to be climbed from two completely different sides in quick succession—by Whymper and his group following the Swiss Ridge, and by Carrel and his friend from the Italian side. The thought that the North Face of the mountain might also be climbable didn't occur to people for more than another fifty years, at a time when solving the problems of the hardest faces and ridges in the Alps was approaching its high point.

And exactly as the summit of the Matterhorn had a special attraction in the peak-bagging era, so too the North Face of this elegant four-thousander exercised a similar magnetic pull to extreme climbers in the classical era of hard Alpinism. It was not just the steepness that was challenging, but also the line.

Today the Matterhorn retains its allure, even when all climbers know that it is loose and certainly not as difficult as it appears. Its logical line, its superlative free-climbing and, above all, the fact that the climb leads directly onto the summit of the mountain, give the Matterhorn North Face route its special reputation.

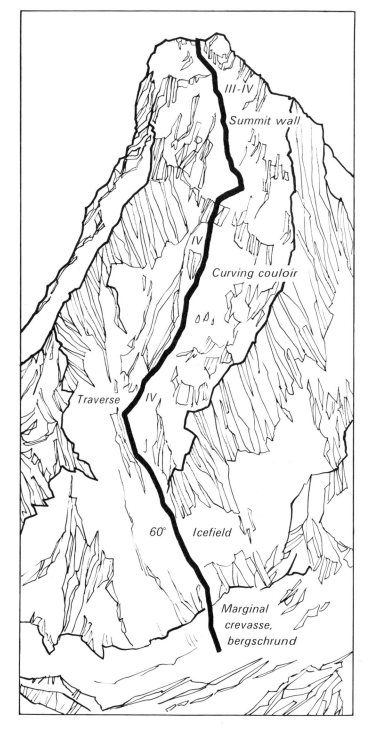

Marginal
crevasse,
bergschrund

(labels on figure) III–IV · Summit wall · IV · Curving couloir · Traverse · IV · 60° · Icefield

Matterhorn North Face, Schmid Route

The first third of the Matterhorn North Face comprises pure ice climbing; what follows is frequently iced-up, unpleasant, stratified rock.

Summit Height: 4,476 m.

Face Height: 1,100 m (between 3,400 m and 4,476 m).

Difficulty: III–IV, relatively broken, 55–60° ice pitches.

Duration: 8–15 hours for a rope under normal conditions and competent in belaying techniques.

Necessary Equipment: Crampons, short axe, a dozen rock and ice pitons (screws). Bivouac equipment. Doubled rope better than single.

Starting Point: The Hörnli Hut (3,260 m), reached from Zermatt by the Schwarzsee Railway and thence by foot.

Route: The great curving couloir in the middle of the face, reached from the left across a steep ice shield, points the way in the austere heart of the face. In the featureless summit slopes, the climber should keep to the right.

Tips: In the early summer the face usually displays the best conditions. Hardly any pitons remain in place, so it is recommended that a selection be taken. The traverse from the icefield to the oblique couloir should not be made too high. A good partnership in normal circumstances will easily complete the climb in a single day. Bivouac sites are small and scarce.

Reinhold Messner has twice attempted the Matterhorn North Face. He had bad luck both times. The first was during the winter of 1965 attempting a second ascent of the Bonatti Route, then in the summer of 1974 he experienced a storm on the Schmid Route. In both cases he came out of it unscathed. The first time back at the start of the climb, the second time on the summit.

When Peter Habeler (both photos) and Reinhold Messner were climbing the Matterhorn North Face in 1974, it snowed almost the whole time. Lightning and stonefalls menaced the summit wall.

The History

When Edward Whymper stood victorious on the summit of the Matterhorn in 1865, he had not only won the struggle for this particular four-thousander, at the same time bringing to an end the West Alpine peak-bagging phase, he also had opened the doors to an increased importance for mountaineering beyond Europe. Technically difficult climbing, which began in the Alps soon after 1865 and reached its peak there seventy years later on the great summits of the Western Alps, was to begin a hundred years later on the world's highest mountains.

From the beginning of Alpinism a hundred years had passed before the Matterhorn could be conquered, and another hundred years of experience were necessary before man could consider attempting the hardest flanks of the eight-thousanders. These Big Walls pose for today's young climbers the same degree of challenge as for instance the Matterhorn North Face held for climbers after the First World War.

At that time a lot was talked about the 'last problems of the Alps' and no less a person than Emil Solleder played with the idea of climbing the Matterhorn North Face. Solleder, a master on rock, lacked experience on ice, as did most other contenders for these last great face problems. To succeed on the Matterhorn it wasn't good enough to be a superb rock climber — condition, hardness, ice technique and not least a facility for route-finding, all played important roles.

There were many who appreciated the problems

and sought to solve them. The two who became the eventual victors were Franz and Toni Schmid. In 1931 they arrived from Munich on their motorcycle and after their successful climb rode home again. The two, after putting the steep icefield behind them, attacked the oblique gully in the centre of the face and bivouaced at the end of it. The glazed rocks were awkwardly stratified and at times broken, and, in addition, on the second day clouds and snow drifts added to their difficulties. It was not until late afternoon that the brothers reached the summit. They knew that they must have been given up for lost since they could not be seen from below, either on the summit or on the descent to the Solvay Hut, where the storm raged on for a long time.

None of the three great Alpine faces has been repeated as often as the Schmid Route on the Matterhorn, but in spite of this, it is not over-pitonned. It is frequently climbed solo (first by Dieter Marchart in 1959) and also in winter (first by Hilti von Allmen and Paul Etter in 1962), and today one can reckon on between 50 and 100 ascents of the route each year by climbers from all over the world — Japan, Spain, America.

With the first ascent of the Direct North Face Route in winter, and moreover solo, Walter Bonatti in 1965 indeed ushered in a new dimension to classical Alpine climbing, but his route — even though it has been repeated several times — does not have the same appeal as the Schmid Route, which remains the 'classic' because it is logical.

A Critical Situation on the Matterhorn

At the end of July 1974
towards 7 o'clock in the morning, Peter Habeler and I stood dubiously at the foot of the Difficult Crack on the Eiger North Face. It was warm and therefore everything was so wet that we couldn't make up our minds whether to go on climbing or not. On the ledges under the first buttress of smooth rock it was so unpleasant that progress came to a sudden halt. Ten paces to our left we were confronted with a serious hazard. Lumps of ice kept crashing down. Waterfalls gushed down the Rote Fluh and it was drizzling above the Hinterstoisser traverse. We gave up and climbed back down the face.

That same evening
we sat in the Hörnli Hut under the Matterhorn trying to engage the guides present in conversation. From them we wanted to learn what sort of condition the North Face was in. Our abortive attempt on the Eiger was already far from our minds. We had climbed down to the valley and come straight on to Zermatt. Climbing up to the hut Peter had set a buoyant pace.

The guides were all of one opinion and that was that although the face was not exhibiting any signs of being in good condition, yet it must be possible. We should allow two days, and a storm in the afternoon, they said, should not be ruled out. This counsel left us a little uneasy and we leafed through the hut book hoping to find a recent entry for the North Face. We didn't find any. Thus we passed the evening in the cheerless room. But just before we went to bed — Peter was already discussing with some young Americans their plans to climb the Normal Route — I met up with a Japanese climber in the outer room who was all equipped in North Wall gear. He was so exhausted that he looked stoned. At first sight I didn't know if he was a junkie or a very hard climber. Hesitantly I asked 'Matterhorn North Face?' He nodded and gave me to understand that it had been very tough. 'The face is all iced-up. We bivouaced at the end of the great couloir — spent the whole night on a tiny ledge. It was bitterly cold, even on the way down.' His companion, another Japanese had joined us in the meantime and beamed broadly when he saw my interest.

This chance meeting
strengthened our resolve to have a go at the North Face the next morning. We checked our equipment that night, put everything we would need for a bivouac into a rucksack, and set the alarm for 2 o'clock.

When we left the hut shortly after 2, we could see from the many glimmering lights that there were already a number of parties on the Hornli Ridge. A Swiss guide making for the Zmutt ridge had begun the traverse under the North Face in front of us. Peter and I — still climbing simultaneously — overtook him, while he was carefully safeguarding his client on a steep ice buttress. The ice was quite blank in places and we were glad when, as we reached the plateau under the North Face, the first grey light dawned.

We stamped our way a few hundred metres further through slushy snow until we were below a place where it looked all right to cross the bergschrund. Directly above us rose a steep ice shield; smooth and unremitting; it led up to the curving couloir and was mostly as hard as iron. We made straight for the crevasse, roped ourselves up and crossed it without difficulty. The ice in the Great Ice Field was glassy and the climbing not without danger, so we had to keep putting in intermediate pitons.

In the meantime the grey clouds which traditionally muffle the summit of the Matterhorn each morning had appeared and masked the surrounding ridges. They clung round the mountain down to about the 4,000 metre mark. Peter and I reached the start of the great traverse very quickly and hoped therefore to be on the summit in a few hours.

The certainty that by late afternoon we would have the North Face behind us mounted as we crossed the last notorious pitches of glazed rocks in the Curving Couloir. Neither of us had felt like stopping so far. Everything had gone smoothly and as free from trouble as if we were on a classic Dolomite climb. We negotiated the steep loose groove without difficulty and came to the spot where the Japanese climbers had bivouaced — marked by a few odds and ends. All this time I had not for a moment felt as if we were on one of the great faces of the Alps. Even after the first snow-flakes had been whirling for an hour or so, we were cheerfully confident, perhaps over-confident.

Not until we reached the steeply sloping slabs which led out to the right across the smooth summit wall, did I suddenly feel that we had begun to lose our advantage. Enough snow had fallen by this time to cover all the little ledges and cracks that were to serve as our foot and hand holds. I was in the lead and called back to warn Peter how difficult everything — friction climbing, construction of belays, to say nothing of free climbing, was becoming. Moreover, I was no longer sure which was the best way to proceed. I looked left and then right — everywhere the same steep precipitous slabs. Under the loose layer of new snow the rocks were coated with a thin layer of ice, which was particularly unpleasant as there were no horizontal footholds anywhere. Worse still — in the middle of a holdless, smooth slope the rope ran out. I was forced to hammer half a dozen knife-blade pitons into two hairline cracks. It was the only way I could construct a reliable belay.

Once he had joined me, Peter climbed on whilst I belayed him, out to the right and then in the thickening

34

One needs courage and self-confidence to climb the Matterhorn North Face when it is iced-up and the weather is uncertain. One also needs to be prepared to turn back.

Somewhere between the Shoulder and the Summit,
Reinhold Messner and Peter Habeler found a spur
relatively free from stonefall danger and were able to
complete their Matterhorn North Face ascent.
Notwithstanding this, conditions could not have
been worse: storms, snow, cold.

snow, back left above me to the edge of a spur of rock.
The original route seemed to take a line out to the right
but was swept by perpetual new snow avalanches and
he therefore had no other choice than this projecting
spur. On it, and it was truly the steepest rock passage
in the vicinity, at least he didn't run the danger of
being swept off into the void by these periodic
avalanches. From my own stance I looked at some
cracks which rose to the left up to the shoulder of the
mountain. Useless. The cracks were channels for
snowslides and out of the question. We had to
concentrate on the rock spur which, steep and forbid-
ding, rose above us.

Centimetre by centimetre

I dragged myself upwards, cleaning off each hold as I
went along. When a snowslide flowed over me like a
waterfall, I would duck, bent almost double, and wait
until the icy shower had passed. Then instinctively I
would begin again, scrabbling with the tips of my
fingers to uncover the holds for the next move. I had
been able to place a few pegs and so the slim hope
grew in me that I might not plunge unchecked if I
suddenly slipped from the icy holds. I thought I
perceived a narrow ledge under the layers of snow and,
holding my breath, I gingerly balanced my way up to
the left.

The few lulls in the storm permitted snatches of
conversation, and whilst I kept saying that I was on the
brink of falling, Peter encouraged me not to give up,
promising that it was only a few more metres up to the
shelter of an overhang. Once there I tried to place
some pegs for a belay and during my seemingly-
everlasting search for cracks, I soon realised that the
standing about was even worse than the climbing. I
was chilled and wet. The fine powder snow which the
storm — now graduated into a hurricane — blew
inside my clothes, was melting against my skin.

Another avalanche rattled down

over me. The overhang, under which we had hoped to shelter, was too small to offer any protection from the cascades of snow that poured down upon us. When Peter had climbed up on a tight rope to join me on my perch, he had warmed up slightly. But the pitches ahead and the continual bombardment of avalanches would drain him despite his reserves. 'I am glad it's you' I said as he climbed on past me to take over the lead, 'I wouldn't care to have anyone else leading just now.' The face was plastered with a layer of ice and snow and every time a flash of lightning struck the summit rocks, we would stiffen and wait for the stones we knew must swiftly follow. They whirred down past us. We were both chilled. A retreat was now out of the question. We laboured up to a spur between the main summit and the shoulder. 'Don't come off now' I heard Peter murmur to himself. He was climbing in a steep gully. Again powder snow avalanches were engulfing him so that for a few minutes at a time I couldn't see him at all. 'Watch out!' he shouted down again. Peter climbed without gloves, hold by hold, in constant danger of coming off; anyone else would surely have fallen, but not he. He inched steadily onwards.

It was not just the rope

that bound us together on this storm-battered summit wall; we were linked in a battle for survival under the constant threat of lightning — wherever it struck it invariably unleashed a hail of stones. Above us, to the side of us, the stone avalanches hurtled down into the depths. It was only our mutual respect that helped us preserve a measure of calm and come safely through the next two pitches.

Suddenly the angle eased, the rock became better jointed and thereby easier to climb. It kept on snowing and the thunder continued to crash all around us, but we could now make out the summit ridge through the cloud and snowdrifts. Soon our hours of battle against the elements would be over.

It was already past midday

when we shook hands on the ridge. Because of the lightning risk we made haste to get off the mountain top as soon as possible.

We climbed down to the Shoulder; from there we could see the complete descent route, which neither of us knew from experience, but which was easily distinguished by the number of parties making their way down. In their bright clothing, they were easy to pick out against the grubby snow-covered rocks.

We enjoyed the descent as much as we had enjoyed climbing the central section of the face some hours before. The guides assisting their clients down step by step, were somewhat surprised when we greeted them from above, having all hoped and assumed that we had given up and retreated when the storm broke. Back in the hut they congratulated us warmly.

The Partner

The right choice of partner for a particular climbing objective is a basic ingredient for its success. The reciprocal trust must be great, especially in critical situations when it can even be a life-saving factor.

In all my climbing career I have not known a better climbing partner than Peter Habeler, and although we have made relatively few climbs together, we have always come out of them in perfect harmony. This is in no small measure due to the fact that Peter is a considerable expert, is always in superlative condition and that we are well-matched — but also it is a result of his essential personality. This is noticeable on a serious climb in all sorts of little ways. Peter is no ditherer; he openly states his opinion and stands by it. He can instinctively gauge the measure of any situation in which he finds himself and can recognise the precise relationship one to another between the people concerned and the circumstances surrounding them.

On a climb intuition can play as important a role as can mental or physical skills. That's certainly true for Peter and I, with the only proviso that on a single climb the situation can sometimes change, and it is the person who is in the lead at the time, who can best appreciate such change. Which of us reaches the summit first will depend on how things develop during the climb. Who is in front and who behind happens spontaneously and can in the space of ten minutes be just as spontaneously reversed.

For the lead to be taken over by whoever is stronger at a particular moment is the logical way to operate a joint venture. It can happen with some people that climbing ambition, or feelings of self-preservation or aggression can disturb the natural balance of a partnership and thus hazard its safety, even the safety of a whole expedition. I am convinced — because I have often experienced it or seen it happen to my friends — that a leader who is in front because he naturally

An ideal partnership: Peter Habeler, left, and Reinhold Messner.

should be, can convert danger into safety. Because we alternate leads like this, without friction, Peter and I have never imposed upon each other and I am sure that this is why we have succeeded on most of our big ventures.

For example, I still remember very well how on the steep Northeast Face of Yerupaja Grande in the Peruvian Andes, Peter took over the lead when I was suddenly overcome by a bout of nausea after taking a glucose tablet.

That we have a sympathetic partnership is also demonstrated by the fact that neither of us has felt the need to criticise the other, or underplay his role, after any of our climbs. How often one gets the impression from climbing reminiscences and attendant gossip that years after a major Alpine enterprise one of the participants is seeking to take more than his share of credit, as if to eclipse his former partner. This is neither dangerous nor important, but it is evidence of the fact that the particular partnership could never have been a harmonious one.

Grandes Jorasses Walker Spur

The North Face of the Grandes Jorasses consists of a series of horizontal rock buttresses, diminishing in height towards the right. They stand tucked away in the heart of the Mont Blanc Massif but were nevertheless discovered by mountaineers quite early. This great granite facade was first sketched, then photographed and in 1935, climbed for the first time. But the ideal route, the Walker Spur, was not accomplished till a few years later; since then it has ranked as 'the most beautiful of the extreme Alpine routes.'

Although today there are more than a dozen routes on the North Face, the Walker Spur remains the classic favourite and whenever the Three Great Alpine Faces are mentioned, one thinks immediately of this imposing face and the granite pillar soaring to the Pointe Walker. Its steepness and compactness give it a special kind of fascination. The lure of the Matterhorn is in its improbable shape, which is mirrored in its North Face; the Eigerwand's attraction is the size and logic of its route; and so with the Walker Spur, it is the elegance and directness of its line which immediately challenges the climber.

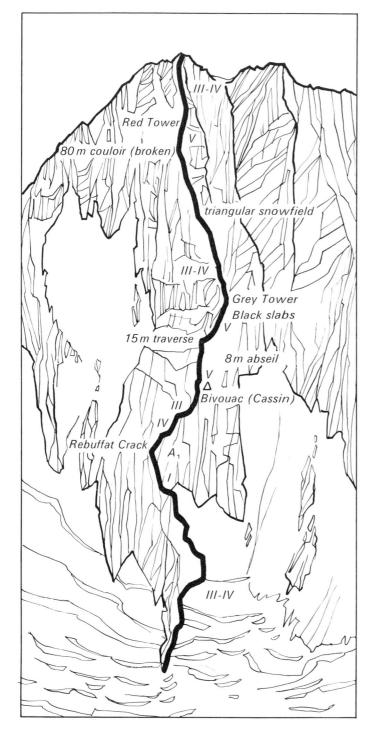

Red Tower

III–IV

V

80 m couloir (broken)

triangular snowfield

III–IV

Grey Tower
Black slabs
V

15 m traverse

8 m abseil

V
△
Bivouac (Cassin)

III

IV

Rebuffat Crack

A₁
I

III–IV

Grandes Jorasses — Walker Spur, Cassin Route

The Walker Spur is principally a rock climb.

Summit height: 4,208 m.

Face height: ca.1,200 m (between 3,000 and 4,208 m).

Difficulty: With the 50 pegs already in place, V–VI, A_1; frequently icy.

Duration: 10–15 hours for a roped party in normal conditions.

Material required: Crampons, short axe or ice hammer, two dozen rock and half a dozen ice pitons (screws), bivouac equipment, double rope.

Starting point: Leschaux Hut (2,431 m), reached from Chamonix (France) via the Montenvers rack-and-pinion railway and the Mer de Glace.

Outline of the Route: The Walker Spur rises compactly and very steeply above the Leschaux Glacier. Above the start the route goes to the left, then straight up and in the summit zone follows to the right of the crest of the spur.

Tips: Although a strong party can complete the Walker Spur in a day, the possibility of a bivouac should always be reckoned with. In badly iced conditions this already difficult route can become very serious indeed. There are a variety of suitable bivouac sites (particularly between 3,900 m and 4,000 m). The wall is notorious for its sudden changes of weather and thunderstorms.

Reinhold Messner was just 20 years old when he climed the Walker Spur on the Grandes Jorasses. It was his first big North Face. Ten years later he became the first and, to date, the only man to have climbed all the 'Big Walls': the Three Big Walls of the Alps and the Three Big Walls of the World.

The History

In the thirties a journey to the Western Alps was as difficult and detailed an operation as an expedition is today. When Gustl Kröner (who was later killed attempting the second ascent of the Matterhorn North Face) and Anderl Heckmair cycled to Chamonix in June 1931 to attempt the Northern precipices of the Grandes Jorasses, they sent their equipment separately as freight. They had to wait around at the foot of Mont Blanc for almost two weeks before their luggage caught up with them, as long as it would take a modern light-weight expedition to accomplish an eight-thousander.

Eager competition to be the first to climb the Jorasses Face had begun a few years earlier. In 1935 it reached an initial conclusion, having by that time already claimed a number of victims, when in the summer of that year Rudolf Peters and Martin Maier completed the first ascent. Their route, however, followed the Croz Spur and didn't finish on the main summit. Meantime, the Walker Spur — already frequently attempted without success — was not forgotten. A second struggle ensued for the contemporary last remaining problem of the Alps.

With his own brand of determination, Riccardo Cassin hurried to the Grandes Jorasses, having been too late for the Eigerwand, and in 1938 with Ugo Tizzoni and Gino Esposito he succeeded in accomplishing the first ascent of what today is known as the most beautiful route in the Alps. It took three days. Riccardo Cassin, without doubt the best climber of his generation, had thereby established a route which in steepness, length and difficulty surpassed that of Peters and Meier.

Today, having received some several hundred ascents and also having been often climbed in winter (firstly by Walter Bonatti and Cosimo Zapelli, 1963) and solo (first by Alessandro Gogna, 1968), the route is considerably over-pegged. The Croz Spur is again becoming popular but will always rank second to the Walker Spur. The same is true of all the other routes that have since been traced across the North Face of the Grandes Jorasses, some of which have required siege tactics, some being undertaken in winter.

Bivouac on the Walker Spur

We had made a lot of plans
for that summer. We had been to the Dolomites to prepare ourselves for the Western Alps and had often discussed the Walker Spur, having seen it described in books as the most beautiful route in the Alps. When Günther, my brother, and I were waiting at Milan station for a connection, several people enquired whether we were returning from Mount Everest — so big were our rucksacks, our faces so sunburnt. For this our first trip to the Western Alps, we had saved for a year and had run many thousands of metres in training. Now we were waiting for the train that would carry us and our many plans, our dreams and hopes, to Courmayeur.

We arrived in torrential rain and the next morning there was still no sight of Mont Blanc through the clouds. Nevertheless we tramped off that day to Chamonix and from there climbed up to the Argentière Hut.

The next morning in youthful innocence, we plodded off towards the foot of the Courtes North Face. Snow purled over the icy slopes and all the other climbers were heading off the mountain in groups. But Günther and I kept on and in four hours reached the summit. We peered through the mist from the highest point, waiting in vain for the wind to drop and the clouds to disperse. We were unlucky, only for a few short moments did we glimpse the North Face of the Grandes Jorasses through the mist. We had already briefed ourselves on the fierce routes on this 1,000 metre-plus face, we carried the image of its rocks and ice deep inside us, and only when the wind and thick mists had again enveloped it, did we begin our descent.

My second trip to the Western Alps
coincided with the fine weather period in the August of 1966. Fresh snow had settled on all the faces but would not, we thought, be any impediment. But the Chamonix guides spoke of poor conditions, particularly of too much new snow in the Argentière Basin and on the Brenva slopes and the Grandes Jorasses. 'The Walker Spur is coated in ice right to its base and is practically impossible', one of the locals informed us. But since we had come to Chamonix with the secret desire of making straight for the Walker, we were at first disinclined to believe him.

For three days we consulted the weather reports. They were so promising it seemed idle to discuss them further. We were intoxicated by the prospect of so many fine days, but didn't know what to do for the best as local opinion continued to advise caution. We decided to take the little railway up to Montenvers so that we could see the condition of the face with our own eyes.

We spent half an afternoon there, gazing at the West Face of the Dru, the Bonatti Spur and the Charmoz North Face but continually coming back to the Jorasses Wall. Although I secretly hankered after the Walker Spur, there was a daunting amount of ice on the upper half of the face and I discussed with Sepp Mayerl and Fritz Zambra, the two climbers from East Tyrol in our group of four, which also included Peter Habeler, the various possibilities for alternative worthwhile routes in the region.

We gathered around a big telescope and every time Peter looked through it, he would adjust it so that when I peered in after him, it would be focused on the notorious Red Chimney on the Walker Spur. It appeared wintry certainly, but the weather was good and, as Peter was at pains to point out, there was nothing else in the whole Mont Blanc area that could remotely compare with the Walker Spur. So it was that an hour later, against the better judgement of our two older members, but full of expectancy, we tramped over the Mer de Glace towards the Leschaux Hut. We would at least make an attempt on the Walker the next day.

Bent under the weight of our rucksacks and morosely contemplating our plan, we continued for a time one behind the other in silence. It was only when we were well up the dead glacier that we all four paused and reflected upon the Cassin Route that appeared whiter and whiter the nearer we approached.

Peter's climbing proficiency

at that time was second to none. He had acquired his Guide's Diploma with Distinction. Even more than with his competence on rock, the authorities had been amazed by his all-round ability and his strict self-discipline. His slim, almost frail physique seemed completely unsuited for extreme tours. Yet once on a face, he was like a cat. His movements radiated confidence and skill. He could climb anything, any kind of terrain be it rock, ice or a mixture of both; he would climb as one of a team or on his own, in summer or in winter. Besides talent, he also had that kind of endurance which can only be achieved by rigid year-round training. In those days I would have backed him to climb anything that even the experts described as 'diabolical'.

Seen from Montenvers, the Mer de Glace looks like an enormous S, thrusting right to the foot of the Grandes Jorasses. On its right stands the Aiguille du Charmoz, its North Face prey to continual stonefalls; to the left the Aiguille du Dru, like a mighty gothic spire carved from the granite of the Aiguille Verte. The crevasses of the glacier were mostly filled with stones and rock, so that to start with we moved forward very quickly. Further up, there were isolated blocks of ice lying on the glacier, and sometimes imposing glacier tables. The sun would melt away the ice around the rocks, so that the rocks — often as big as the room of a house — would be left perched on slender ice cones like monster mushrooms of rock and ice.

During the late afternoon we reached the bivouac shelter on the right bank of the glacier, the Walker Spur soaring immediately above us.

It was still dark when we left the shelter the next morning. An icy wind caught us in the face as we opened the door, and the rocks in front of the hut were coated with thick rime. In the cone of light from our pocket lamp, we looked for the start of the climb and had to jump over crevasses, negotiate our way round seracs, and were glad that, when we reached the bergschrund, it was already beginning to get light. We made good progress on the crisp firn and for a moment

On the iced slabs at the beginning of the Walker Spur, the four men Habeler-Mayerl-Zambra-Messner met far greater difficulties than on the vertical section in the middle of the face. During the climb Peter Habeler (photo left) and Reinhold Messner learned to appreciate each other's climbing. Since then they have become one of the most successful teams since the War.

seriously debated whether we need rope up at all. But one does conventionally rope up at the start of a big climb like this and we accepted the sense of it, and climbed roped — Fritz and I on the first rope, Peter and Sepp following behind. Everything went well so long as we bypassed the isolated patches of rock in the icefield, or made use of them purely for belays.

But higher up

the ice slope was bisected by a rock barrier with a few extremely steep patches of ice clinging between the rocks. The ice was glassy and hard, often only a thin layer on top of smooth granite slabs and it would ring hollowly when I struck it with my axe.

There were two possibilities open to us now if we were to make further progress — we had either to climb the rocks or the thin ice that coated them. We first tried scraping off the armour of ice to reach the rock; with a loud splintering sound, the fragments came away and clattered down the mountain, and having climbed that small section then we had once more to start paring off the formidable ice plaque. Next we tried front-pointing on our crampons, performing a delicate and not undangerous dance on the thin ice.

With each metre we climbed, the steepness of the face increased. Soon the only ice remaining was deep inside the cracks and crevices, and once, at the end of a crack, I had to make six attempts before I could climb out onto the platform above, each time sinking back to my last hold.

Exhausted, I made for the Rebuffat Crack. In the meantime Peter and Sepp had taken over the lead. In these wintry conditions we would only make good progress if we divided the work between us in a friendly fashion. The so-called 75-metre dièdre at the end of the first third of the face, was so choked with ice inside that all the existing pegs were buried beneath it.

Peter Habeler in the Rebuffat Crack on the North Face of the Grandes Jorasses . . . some doubt as to the way ahead.

Straddling the crack widely, Sepp climbed up and then handed the lead over to Peter, each giving of his best.

It was night before the last of us reached the Cassin Bivouac at the end of the pendulum traverse. It was a very clear, bright, starry night and the temperature was correspondingly low. On two steep ledges we sat close together, two and two, and waited for the morning. After the hazards and exertions of the past day, the whirl of tension and anxiety, uncertainty and necessity, it was a wonder that we had come through it so well, and we began to doze in our bivouac sacks. But the wind with curious persistency found its way through our layers of clothes and kept tearing us out of our half-sleep.

My gaze ranged over ridges, glaciers,
crazy needles of rock to the valley beyond . . . it was all strange, distant and somehow inconsequential, silhouettes which in my mind it seemed I had seen before. This then was the Walker Spur, and this was me sitting here, freezing cold and with my toes gone to sleep. No way off now. We should have enough pegs and ice screws to get us to the top.

The feeling spread in me that for the time being we were safe, because like it or not there was nothing we could do here in the bivouac at night, it was a comforting thought but at the same time disturbing. My whole body craved warmth and rest. But the continuing night was like a blanket on which I sat. I didn't sleep, I didn't shut my eyes any more, tiredness weighed like lead in my arms and legs. I had the uneasy feeling and it struck me again in the early hours of the morning — that I could no longer think what I wanted to think, had no power over my thoughts. They wandered at will and despite my resistance always harked back to the unnerving prospect of steep, glazed slabs, chimneys packed with compressed snow, vertical

Nearing the top of the Walker Spur. Snow, ice, oncoming darkness. The summit within sight.

spurs. It drove me to despair. Perhaps it was the lack of sleep and the cold — it was already getting light — or perhaps it was the long inactivity that crippled my will, like sleep a dreaming body.

This limbo between sleeping and waking dispersed once I had put the first rope's length behind me. We climbed the slabs of the Tour Grise, the grey tower, and the subsequent rock crest faster than we expected that morning. The wind had helped, the sharp rocks were clear of snow, and it was only when we reached the ice field above that our resources were really tested. We lost so much time putting on and taking off our crampons that when we reached the Red Chimney we scarcely hoped to reach the summit the same day.

Wearily we sought the route
upwards. We gave up trying to find the pegs under the sheath of ice and hammered in our own instead. How tiring it was! When all is said and done — if one knew from the start just how desperately tiring it is to climb the Walker Spur when it is completely iced-up, one would gladly wait for good conditions, even if it took several years!

It was all the more rewarding, therefore, when in the late hours of the afternoon of the same day, our hands clutched the rocks of the Pointe Walker, the summit.

We were happy enough to bivouac during our descent down the other side, knowing that we should reach the hut the following day. In the night it snowed and at regular intervals the heaped snow would slide off our bivouac sacks; whenever I moved, the wind blew a fine powder of snow under the nylon cover.

Again we froze, the moisture creeping under our clothes. We didn't care to struggle with the stove and got moving before it was light. Because of the threat of avalanches after such a heavy snowfall, we wanted to be well clear of the mountain and get down to the valley early.

Success

I have often been asked why so much envy and mistrust exists among climbers. This observation, in itself unimportant, is only valid if a mountain climber is seen as an individualist who spends his free time in the mountains. Even then one might have supposed that he would be happy that other people had discovered the same fascination in his sport as he had, and that any Alpine achievement represented an enrichment to Alpinism generally.

It is interesting to observe that jealousy does not exist among the absolute top climbers; it shows itself mainly between climbers of different abilities. My own feeling is that it is the lack of overt competition in mountaineering that produces it. Climbers of real ability don't need this kind of identity prop, don't need to compare themselves to anyone else, nor indeed do any people of common sense. And note too, that we are not here talking about the 'best', but purely about the 'successful' Alpinist. For successes are all one can measure, and because these are not entirely dependent upon ability, conflict can often break out between two or more mountaineers or between groups of mountaineers.

Activity, skill and finance are all factors that influence a climber's success. Activity may be the result of keenness and vitality; skill, of aptitude, training and practical experience; but the climber's financial resources are obviously dependent on his position and occupation. In the early days it was only well-off people who climbed mountains and only a hundred years ago the Viennese climber, Paul Grohmann, devoted a whole fortune to conquering the most important Dolomite summits.

Today climbing is possible for a much broader section of society and is more a question of time than of money. For example, anyone who wants to take part in a big expedition has got to be able to take at least three months off work, longer than the usual holiday allocation — so in consequence, he must work twice as hard for the rest of the year. For my own part I have chosen the uncertain path of having no career outside of climbing to ensure the greatest independence and mobility in order to undertake big expeditions anywhere at any time.

The fact that a climber's success depends on so many factors is to some extent delightful, but it does admit a charlatan-element which can bear strange fruit. A mountaineering-charlatan is someone who takes part in a trekking holiday in Nepal and lets people think he has been on a Himalayan expedition. A charlatan is someone who gives his readers or listeners the impression that he has climbed Nanga Parbat when he hasn't himself gone high. A charlatan is someone who, when he makes the first ascent of a Grade IV climb, bestows a grade VI upon it.

It would be interesting to discover whether jealousy among the many success-oriented climbers persisted if the example of climbers in Lombardy (Italy) were followed. They hold a competition which takes account of year-round, world-wide climbing activity. By the award of this 'Grignetta d'oro' — as it is called — the climber with the worthiest tour record each year is honoured. A certain number of routes and their difficulties are taken into account; participants are graded according to age, and anyone who has a fall is excluded (this clause was adopted by the competition authorities largely on my recommendation). The routes are allocated points commensurate with their severity and as far as the Alps are concerned, it is the Walker Spur that carries the most points.

The Grignetta d'oro competition, besides encouraging the discipline of weighing up risk, is an attempt to directly compare the achievements of various Alpinists. Annual contests of this kind have been secretly taking place locally for decades — one has only to look up the many tour records and periodicals that clubs and associations publish to see this is so. All young men seem to need this sort of competition amongst themselves and one should not be surprised to discover it amongst climbers also. In any other top sport, the competitive element is taken for granted — only in mountaineering is it considered taboo.

I am not trying to say that I would like to see an International Climber of the Year Award to go to the most successful Alpinist in the same way as a world cup goes to the top Alpine skier, I am merely suggesting that perhaps such open competition could eliminate a lot of the in-fighting that now goes on in the climbing world.

An Alpine competition would recognise such qualities as competence, resolve, commitment, self-discipline, enthusiasm, facility for comradeship — all traditionally ingredients on which the success of a climber has depended. Such a competition would not only rank climbing as a very individual and wide-ranging sport, it would certainly be less dangerous than 'competitive parallel climbing' which has been suggested as an Olympic sport, where for example, ten ropes would launch themselves wildly on the Walker Spur at the same time. The fastest wins.

. . . If he doesn't fall off first, I would add, for I know something of the risks of competition. The mass media and an entertainment-hungry public would be glad to see this kind of 'race' — it is the climbers who do not want it. Let us hope that climbers of the future don't let themselves in for such stupidity either.

The more commonplace pressure that publicity exerts is less dangerous. 'Don't take offence' one is earnestly requested 'if we are always on the look-out for something new. You must appreciate how record-holders in any sport, including climbing, are under continual pressure to improve on their achievements. Of course it's unfair but that's how life is, sadly'. Challenges like this are always being made to me in the hope of some new sensation. Even my own club

Reinhold Messner on the Walker Spur, 1966.

friends are constantly waiting for me to produce bigger and better successes.

It may be that in the past I have been influenced by this sort of outside stimulus in my choice of some climb or other. But when it comes to a crisis, it is not pressure from publicity, nor prospect of gain, nor yet press or television contracts that drive me on, but an elemental desire to reach the summit, or, quite simply, to survive.

49

The Eiger North Face

With any luck, all the notoriety that has surrounded the Eiger North Face as a result of the dramatic struggle for its first ascent, coupled with the many tragedies of the fifties and sixties, is now past. For a quarter of a century, this was the most infamous rock climb in the world; now, amongst climbers at least, it is considered to be just one of the great West Alpine faces, even if in popular folk-lore it remains the epitome of suicidal Alpinism.

Success on the far bigger faces of the eight-thousanders — flanks which are more than double the height and in places more difficult than the Eigerwand — have obviously contributed towards the scaling-down of this face in people's minds. Even so, the Eigerwand should never be underestimated.

Viewed from Kleine Scheidegg, the North Face, which according to Professor Brückner is the highest mountain wall in the Alps, exercises a strong fascination. The strange, steep cliff with its icefields one atop the other, certainly appears impregnable, but its structure does dictate the line of the classical route so clearly that today's accomplished climbers still want to repeat it. Apart from the broken rocks before the Difficult Crack and the flat summit icefield, there is no let-up for the climber throughout the entire length of the face. He needs his wits about him the whole time. The continual alternation between rock and ice climbing, the fact that the face is always wet, the stonefall hazard and the abrupt and violent storms for which the Eiger is well known, all these contribute to a certain relentlessness on the part of the mountain. No other West Alpine Face so justly deserves the title of 'a big mixed climb' as does the Eigerwand.

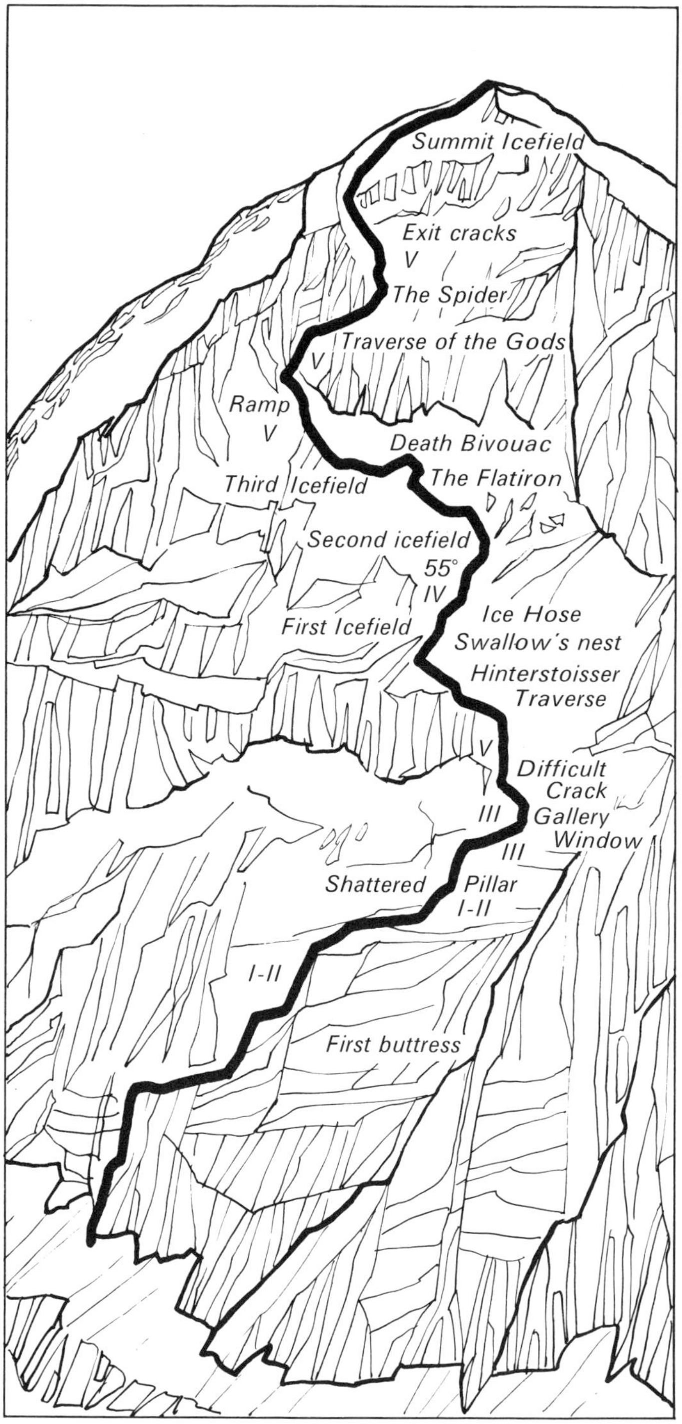
Summit Icefield
Exit cracks
V
The Spider
Traverse of the Gods
V
Ramp
V
Death Bivouac
Third Icefield
The Flatiron
Second icefield
55°
IV
First Icefield
Ice Hose
Swallow's nest
Hinterstoisser
Traverse
V
Difficult
Crack
III
Gallery
Window
III
Shattered
Pillar
I-II
I-II
First buttress

Eiger North Face, Heckmair Route

The continual change between ice and rock passages characterise this climb.

Summit height: 3,970 m.

Face height: ca. 1,800 m (between 2,200 and 3,970 m).

Difficulties: IV–V, generally wet and icy, 50–55° ice slopes.

Duration: 10–20 hours in normal conditions.

Material required: Crampons, short axe, at least two dozen rock and ice pitons (screws), spare clothing, bivouac equipment, double rope.

Starting point: Alpiglen or better still, Kleine Scheidegg (2,061 m) reached by rack-railway from Grindelwald.

Outline of the Route: The route of the first ascent begins in the right hand section of the concave face, traverses out left from the Rote Fluh to the upper edge of The Ramp, turns back towards the centre of the face again immediately above the Ramp Icefield. From here (The Spider) it bears left to the summit ice field.

Tips: The face is well-pitonned and the Swiss Aerial Rescue Service demonstrates a remarkable preparedness to assist climbers in trouble; despite this the face calls for such qualities as practical experience, good ropework and, above all, top condition. The route in places offers really enjoyable climbing and is nowhere extremely difficult, but it can become practically impossible in icy conditions. Because of the danger of stonefall, the icefields and The Spider should not be undertaken during the afternoon. Safe bivouac spots exist at the Flatiron or to the right of the upper edge of the Ramp Icefield. In the event of a storm, it is best to retreat down out of the Ramp.

The Eiger North Face, seen from Kleine Scheidegg. ▷

The History

'Smooth and absolutely unclimbable' — that was how the Englishman, A. W. Moore, described the Eiger North Face in 1864. He had just completed the third ascent of the mountain by its Northwest Ridge, a route which offers a very good view across the North Face. The Eiger had first been climbed in 1858 by Charles Barrington with the guides Christian Almer and Peter Bohren; and it went on to be ascended by its various ridges and slopes before a small group of élite Alpinists began to even consider the possibility of attempting the North Face. Willo Welzenbach was one of the first to give serious thought to the problem in those early days, but he was unable to put his plans into action before he perished on Nanga Parbat. Welzenbach, although he was not a superlative rock climber, combined all those other attributes that are necessary for success on a face like the Eigerwand — he was competent with up-to-date techniques on rock and ice, he was calm and strong, had staying power and previous experience of big faces; he also had a talent for comradeship.

Fatal consequences followed several attempts until in 1937 Hias Rebitsch and Ludwig Vörg succeeded in retreating safely from the Death Bivouac and demonstrated that withdrawal in bad weather was possible. In the midsummer of 1938 Anderl Heckmair, Ludwig Vörg, Fritz Kasparek and Heinrich Harrer completed the first ascent in four days. They encountered a fierce storm on the summit wall and Heckmair put his last ounce of effort into leading the four-man party — two Germans, two Austrians — safely up. The aura that had built up around the face during the dramatic attempts for a first ascent did not die however; after the Second World War the route received its first repeat ascent, but other attempts continued to exact a toll of life. Even after the first winter ascent by Toni Kinshofer, Walter Almberger, Anderl Mannhardt and Toni Hiebeler in 1961, and the first solo ascent by Michael Darbellay in 1963, the face continued to be the most feared in the Alps.

During the seventies, however, the Heckmair route has been repeated many times and the event now passes without much attention; the Eiger has lost some of its sinister reputation. The success of helicopter operations in rescuing climbers in distress has also contributed to a lessening of the mountain's 'killer' image — at least in informed circles.

With every successful ascent, the Eigerwand grows 'smaller', but it is the modern air rescue facilities that more than anything have lessened the scale of its challenge.

Nevertheless — and notwithstanding two important new routes on the face (the Harlin-Direttissima of Winter 1966 and the not-so-logical Japanese Summer Direct route of 1969) — it is the Heckmair Route that remains the 'classical', the ideal line on the Eiger North Face.

Eight Years — and Ten Hours for the Eigerwand

It would crop up in conversation
over and over again. For eight years after our shared days on the Walker Spur, the ambition hung in the air — the Eiger North Face. Its name would emerge in letters between us, in telephone conversations or whenever we happened to meet.

The first attempt was frustrated before the journey across Austria to Switzerland had even begun. 'Eugen schläft — komme nicht, Peter' (Eugen sleeps — don't come, Peter) was the cryptic text of a telegram delivered to me by the Italian Post one day. A somewhat remarkable message from the usually so level-headed Peter Habeler, but after some deliberation it reluctantly dawned on me that it must mean 'Eiger schlecht' (Eiger condition bad) — don't come'.

Our second attempt too
came to naught as a result of a telegram misinterpretation, only this time it was not the fault of the Italian Post but our own. I winged a message to Peter 'Meeting Place Grindelwald Grund Eiger' and set off. At the valley station of the Eiger Railway to Kleine Scheidegg — it's called Grindelwald Grund — I waited a whole day fruitlessly and in despair for Peter who was usually so reliable. At the same time, back in Grindelwald itself, Peter was wandering about the spruce little village, equally sour — as I was to discover days later. He had thought it highly superfluous to give the reason for (Grund) a visit to Grindelwald as the Eiger, but he had never heard of the station Grindelwald Grund. Like me he was vexed by the lost days. Much at the same time, we sadly made our separate ways home.

In the summer of 1969, in which from a climbing point of view I was in better form than at any time before or since, I came twice more to Grindelwald. Once with Erich Lackner on the way back from an international climbing meet in Chamonix and the second time alone. On the first occasion we were driven away by rain and snow, but on my second, solo, visit the weather was fine and I went to Kleine Scheidegg. Fritz von Almen advised me against a lone attempt but the conditions were good. So I started to climb. However during the night I turned back because the parties ahead of me were continually dislodging stones which rattled down alarmingly in the darkness, until I feared I should be caught up in their uncontrollable flight. The objective dangers present on the Eiger make a solo climb a critical enterprise, because, however much the relatively minor difficulties and especially the very long pitches are an obvious attraction to the solo climber, he cannot by himself take sufficient precautionary measures and the smallest stonefall could knock him off. In fact the stonefall hazard made such an impression on me that my ambition to climb the Eigerwand was squeezed into the background. Several years went by during which I was often away on expeditions, and I didn't bother myself too much about it. Then, with growing experience, I came to realise that on a face like the Eigerwand it was speed that really counted, and once again it began to seem a worthwhile prospect. The terrible stonefalls begin in the early afternoon when the sun, shining on the summit wall, loosens the ice that normally binds all the loose stones together. Another advantage of a fast team is that it can effect an escape from that other Eiger hazard — the sudden storm — either by going up, or down.

Peter Habeler had reached a similar conclusion, so we agreed to put our theory to the test. In the summer of 1974 we went three times to Grindelwald before all the prerequisites for a safe climb were right. The first time was in July — and in order to make no mistake about it this time, we came together — and we climbed as far as the Difficult Crack. But waterfalls were pouring down the whole face and we were forced to turn back. We climbed down and that same day went on to Zermatt to attempt the Matterhorn North Face. A week later we were back in Kleine Scheidegg once more, our rucksacks packed, the weather fine. But after our evening meal a grey veil was gradually drawn across the clear sky. By 3 o'clock in the morning clouds obliterated everything, and by 5, it was raining in torrents. Again we went down. Masking our disappointment, we jokingly made an appointment for the next fine weather period.

This came on 14 August 1974

At last everything clicked at once. The face was certainly very wet and it might have been better to wait two or three days, but the weather forecast was good. Three parties were already climbing on the face and they were moving only slowly, so the conditions up there must still be poor. They were making progress, however. That evening we had a chat with Martin Boysen, Dougal Haston and other climbers with a filming party who were shooting scenes for the Hollywood thriller 'The Eiger Sanction'. Haston, at that time the top British climber, described the bad conditions on the face and recommended we wait a little longer. Peter and I wanted to at least make an attempt the next day, however, so we packed our rucksacks with climbing gear, bivouac essentials, and food for two or three days. One never knows . . .

Frau von Almen, our good angel, had sent us off well fortified by a good breakfast in the hotel below — tea, coffee, bread, butter, cheese, marmalade — we still appreciate the comforts of hotel life . . .

An hour later we sat on a grassy bank immediately underneath the face. It was still too dark to start climbing, and we could not make out the outline of the route. We waited for morning which had already announced itself on the eastern horizon. The wall above us was still a great, featureless mass; one would only be able to distinguish between snow and rock on the spot. The lights of Grindelwald were still clearly visible and switching my gaze from the village 1,000 metres below, immediately to the towering hulk some 2,000 metres above us, it seemed doubly dangerous.

Suddenly we thought we saw a light flashing in the middle of the vast face — yes, there it was again; it must be up about the Second Icefield. I counted the seconds between the individual flashes — 21, 22 . . . 29 — and again the tiny light appeared. Was someone in trouble? The signal was repeated: the Alpine distress signal! Should we go back and raise the alarm? We deliberated. Then we began climbing up the scree, ice and snow to the start of the climb. We were well equipped and would be able to help if necessary: our rucksack medicine kit was well stocked and we had plenty of pegs to abseil down to the Gallery Window with an injured man. We started up the face along a ledge to the left of the first pillar.

By this time it was 5 a.m. and light. Waterfalls cascaded over us, and in the Hotel Kleine Scheidegg opposite the first lights were going on. The loose debris of stones and old snow on the ledge called for our full concentration, but otherwise the technical difficulties were slight and the route-finding simple as we already knew this section of the face. We quickly gained the crest of the first pillar above the loose snow and rock, and traversed obliquely out to the right and — still unroped — climbed upwards to the right of the cleft spur.

We only stopped briefly when we reached the bottom of the Difficult Crack. We divided up the Karabiners, ice and rock pegs, and fixed them to our climbing harnesses, put on the many slings and loops, and roped up with the 50 m rope. Bivouac equipment and provisions remained for the time being in the rucksacks.

A rope was already in place, left by the film crew

who had been shooting their spy-thriller, which made things easier for us. Soon we were standing at the lower end of the Hinterstoisser Traverse, over which water was continually sluicing. The rocks above us were smooth and wet but not completely vertical, below us the face was overhanging.

I crossed more snow and ice debris and reached the righthand edge of a flight of slabs that separated us from the First Icefield. Some tattered fragments of old rope bore witness to earlier dramatic retreats and showed us the way. Quickly I traversed to the left — anything rather than get too wet! — and reached a niche where I waited for Peter to join me. Water ran down the overhanging rock and poured over my shoulders, my rucksack and helmet. Soon my clothes were soaked through and heavy.

Without stopping, Peter took over the lead. Over wet rock, small ice patches and vertical steps of rock we climbed, alternating leads, until we reached the lower edge of the Second Icefield. A rock step lay between us and the icefield. Just above us somewhere must be the party whose distress signal we had seen earlier in the morning. Were they still there? Did they need help? We had agreed between us to descend with them if necessary.

We mounted the last vertical upswing of rock to the icefield. We were keeping to the rocks for as long as possible because although they tilted outwards and were streaming with water, at least it was possible to place a few pegs.

Suddenly above me I heard Peter say something. Obviously he was talking to the climbers — they were two Poles — who were in trouble. Peter offered our help but they shook their heads, they felt sure the helicopter would soon arrive.

The ice-glazed Exit Cracks of the Eiger North Face cost the Habeler-Messner rope at least an hour. Safety was more important than a new record, and they took no risks.

That very moment the droning of a helicopter engine could be heard. I had not really appreciated till then just what is involved when a man on a wire rope jumps from the cabin and swings around in nothingness. For a moment the helicopter hovered about 30 metres above the distressed climbers, a few stones loosened by the down draught of the rotor blades squealed past me, then the craft buzzed away from the face. A single stone would be enough to upset the balance of the helicopter, a single stone . . . Meanwhile the rescuer had secured himself between the two Poles and set to work splinting the leg of one of the young men, broken the previous day in a 40 metre fall.

Peter and I had hardly climbed another pitch before the helicopter was back above the three men, its rope dangling. The Swiss rescuer attached the injured man to the rope and signalled with his hand. Immediately the helicopter drew away from the face again. It was well clear of the mountain before the man was hoisted into the machine and whisked off to Kleine Scheidegg. We were so impressed by the whole operation that we shouted our congratulations to the rescue man who now had to wait with the uninjured Pole for the third flight.

On this awesome cliff, 1,000 metres above the meadows, everything had been carried out with such speed and precision that we could only be amazed. Had these techniques been available then, many of the victims claimed by this face in its 40-year climbing history, could certainly have been saved. But for them there was nothing like this . . .

Meanwhile we again put on our crampons and climbed straight up over blank ice to the upper rim of the Second Icefield which afforded some protection from stonefall. The ice screws at the belays held well — all the same I was glad when the helicopter had been back and fetched the other two men, because the danger of stonefall was much greater when the machine flew close.

Traversing around the upper rim of the icefield was a long job, bringing with it no increase in height. We had to be specially careful here because of the threat of falling stones even though the showers were mostly intermittent. We chose stances with some protection and climbed quickly with our ears pricked; at the least suspicion of sound we could take evasive action. Long icicles hung like swords of Damocles over our heads, and now and then a batch of stones from The Spider, which was now directly above us, would hurtle down to the ice below.

The lower limit of frost that day was 3,400 metres, which was a great advantage. When the upper half of the face is in sunshine, all hell must be let loose, I thought, whilst Peter led the last few pitches from the Flatiron to the Death Bivouac. During the afternoon it would be suicidal madness to climb here.

It was still early morning about 9 a.m. when we traversed from the Third Icefield, black with fallen stones, to the Ramp. The face was still relatively quiet. Four Austrians, who had already spent three days on the face, were climbing safely and steadily above us. They had made their first bivouac in the Swallow's Nest, their second at the Flatiron, from where they had set off that morning. Peter knew them well, and they readily let us overtake them.

Peter and I paused to chat about the route ahead with the first rope of Tyrolians at the lower limit of the glassy-hard Ramp Icefield. It led over a broken band to a vertical step, above which must be the start of the Traverse of the Gods. We wished the Austrians luck, hoping to see them in Kleine Scheidegg that evening, and traversed the icefield obliquely outwards to the right.

Above the broken crack we sought to get onto the Traverse of the Gods. We were soaked through, for water had poured down the Ramp in a steady stream, but as we had moved through it so quickly, it had hardly bothered us at all. We progressed pitch after pitch, belaying in turns, and by midday we stood in The Spider. A view up to the summit wall made us hesitate. The sun was still hidden and the rocks looked black and shiny, the cracks and chimneys were full of snow. The Exit Cracks were also iced up. The maze of cracks overhead seemed more extensive than I had expected. Moreover, we knew well enough that in this condition, the summit wall was practically impossible to free-climb. Further over to the right hung some old bits of rope which must surely have been there since the first winter direttissima. But of our own route we could see no immediate clue as to which way we should go. Were we too far to the left or were all the pegs hidden under the coating of ice?

On a sloping stance practically above the Spider, Peter and I held a conference about what to do next. Should we wait here till the sun had melted the thin glaze from the holds and steps, or should we make the most of the last hours of relative freedom from stonefall and, despite the increased level of difficulty, climb on? We decided to do just that. We had faith in each other and so the second alternative was certainly much safer for us. It is very comforting in such a situation to have an excellent partner, one you know will recognise and appreciate the danger, but not let it overawe him. I knew that Peter would not be unnerved, he was always so self-possessed, that together we should reach the summit safely. This trust enabled me to contemplate attempting the frozen summit wall with equanimity.

The first pitch in the Exit Cracks was not excessively steep. Peter climbed, as he had throughout, as if he was out for a ramble and without a moment's hesitation. The next pitch, however, a completely iced-up crack which I was to lead, was a much harder proposition. I kept thinking of Hermann Buhl who had fallen off several times at this point. It was only with difficulty that I could keep my grip on holds which first had to be freed of ice by the warmth of the fingers, and my calves ached sorely from having to stand so long on single footholds no wider than a finger. At the beginning of the crack I had been able to hammer in a reliable peg, but now I had no free hand for putting in pegs. Each movement I tried out several times, for every time I was about to transfer my weight, I would feel as if I was about to slip off and would hold back. To retreat would be relatively easy since the preceding holes were free of ice, but ahead each move carried the risk of a fall if it was not very calmly and deliberately executed. Peter encouraged me to keep on trying and eventually it 'went'. Since this key passage had taken so much out of me, Peter led the next two. He straddled over overhangs, found the occasional old rusty peg and would shout down, assuring me we were on the right route. Alternating leads, we climbed on, the rock becoming less steep.

I thought of my wife who was waiting for us down in Kleine Scheidegg and would surely be watching through the telescope right now. 'If we reach the summit icefield in the early afternoon', I had told her as we left 'you can get the bath-tub ready'. Now I hummed to myself, belayed to my stance 'Get the bath-tub ready!'

It was almost 2 o'clock when for the first time a portion of the wall came into sunshine. Already the first stones began to fall and the chimneys and cracks turn into little watercourses. I saw how small stones and icicles set in motion by the melted water, would jump — I might almost say playfully — down the broken summit slopes and, joined by others, would jostle along with them and tumble down into The Spider as little stone avalanches. Below they rolled over the steep, blank ice and hurtled as formidable

Reinhold Messner (centre) and Peter Habeler (right) after their Eiger climb with the stars of 'The Eiger Sanction' at Kleine Scheidegg. Front left Clint Eastwood, between the two Alpinists Heidi Brühl; behind, from left, Jean Pierre Bernard, Rainer Schöne, Michael Grimm.

projectiles down to the Third and Second Icefields.

We climbed roped for another 100 metres and then untied ourselves and moved together up the last few steps of the face and onto the summit icefield. Now we were free of the stonefalls and would not need to belay any more.

At 3 o'clock we sat on the Eiger summit, the weather still fine, the world around us peaceful and beautiful. Already the stonefalls were forgotten.

Exactly ten hours

had been taken to climb the face. As we left the summit we were, however, less proud of our speedy ascent than of the fact that our timetable had enabled us to elude the falling stones almost completely. The West Ridge was snowed-up in places so that we had to abseil down.

Back at the foot of the face

my wife was waiting for us with hot tea. She had followed the whole climb through Frau von Almen's big telescope and smilingly told us how the film crew would keep interrupting their shooting to peer through the glass as well. And indeed when we reached the hotel, they all pressed around to congratulate us on our new 'Record Time'. They wanted to know all the details but Peter and I disappeared first for the hot bath we had promised ourselves.

At half past five we sat, all clean and tidy, in front of the hotel at Kleine Scheidegg and watched the many people peering through the telescopes at the face. The four Austrians were now climbing the upper exit cracks, and further down, immediately below the Rote Fluh, some other ropes were looking for somewhere dry to bivouac.

Over their ice cream sundaes the film's stars — amongst them Clint Eastwood, Heidi Brühl and Rainer Schöne — had discovered a basic fact about climbing. For the purposes of their film work, they had attended climbing courses and now they found they wanted to do more climbing, they had found it so fascinating. Peter and I celebrated our ascent with the film team and discussed with Norman Dyhrenfurth, their technical advisor, his plans for his next expedition. The sun was no longer strong but pleasantly warm and we did not feel especially tired; we planned our journey home for the following day.

Peter and I were once more hotel guests

as we had been at the same time the day before. When I kept glancing between the two buildings which offered a clear view of the Eigerwand, the face looked mysteriously inviting, as if I hadn't climbed it at all yet. But Peter was rubbing his cheek with a wry smile, the delectable Heidi Brühl had rewarded him with a kiss.

Records

There has frequently been much talk of a 'Record Climb' in connection with our 10 hour ascent of the Eigerwand. Not from us, but from the Press. Peter and I didn't climb the Eiger in 10 hours to set up any new record but in order to eliminate a large proportion of the danger. The 10 hours were just a natural extension of that.

A long time ago it was prophesied that the Eiger North Face would become a race track, with the increasing danger that it would provide the setting for competitive Alpinism. Straight away, therefore, I would like to emphasise that the danger of falling stones is infinitely less in the hours before noon, and that within the space of ten hours the weather is unlikely to reverse completely, provided of course that one starts climbing when the forecast is good.

Olivier Juge, mathematician, top climber and son of the former president of the UIAA, Jean Juge, was one of the few who immediately grasped the significance of these facts. He congratulated us with the words 'Until now I have never been interested in climbing the Eiger, simply because of the objective dangers. Now I wouldn't mind having a go at it, your style.'

I do not believe that climbing is degenerating into mere record-seeking, but I have come round to the conviction that future generations of climbers will be better trained, not only to be able to attempt harder routes, but also because with improved condition, some measure of control over many objective dangers can be exercised. An intensive training is more important for extreme climbing than for any other sport. A thoroughly-trained high-jumper may perhaps win a competition, but a thoroughly-trained climber might extricate himself from a situation in which he would otherwise have perished.

And it is naturally much more satisfying to climb the Eiger as quickly and safely as possible, than to take three or four days over it. I have absolute sympathy for the party that takes several days because it encounters an unexpected storm or has to stop because of an accident, but I venture to suggest that a party requiring more than two days to climb the face in normal conditions, is in no sense ready for such a route. What is needed here is an about-face in popular thinking, for it simply is not heroism when unqualified people with insufficient preparation venture onto such big and dangerous faces and find themselves faced with a life-or-death struggle.

It is equally questionable when climbers are celebrated for their falls. There are climbers who have 'peeled off' many times — to my mind this just exhibits a death-wish philosophy. I can smile at so much nonsense because I have never yet come off whilst leading on a serious face — in the same way that I smile when someone dismisses extreme climbing on the pretext that it is too dangerous. Serious climbing is not intrinsically more or less dangerous than easy climbing, if one is competent for it. I am certain that many climbers on the Normal Route of the Anteleo, to take a single example, risk far more than Peter Habeler and I risked on our Eiger North Face ascent.

So long as climbing Big Walls is dictated by a desire to modify the element of risk and not merely to break records, then it is a justifiable pursuit. Climbing against the clock, as practised in Eastern European countries, may be amusing in itself and it can produce records without danger because the climber is secured on a tight top rope. But serious climbing as I understand it, doesn't enjoy any unnatural help from above. It can only take place on big mountain faces. And any attempt to make or break records for their own sake is — on a Big Wall — dicing with death and not acceptable.

Aconcagua South Face

The South Face of Aconcagua remained for many years unknown amongst German-speaking mountaineers although it was one of the first of the Big Faces of the world to be considered climbable. Even today it has only received a few ascents.

Several kilometres wide at its base and standing three kilometres high, it towers over the Horcones Glacier, encircled by a bleak landscape of snowfields rubble and dead glaciers. The face is continually swept by avalanches and, tucked away as it is in the remotest corner of the Horcones Valley, its complete isolation and the constant wind merely accentuate its wild and menacing aspect. But only the view from the top looking down at the giant bow of the glacier, reveals the true and awesome magnitude of this face.

Despite its steepness and overall difficulty, this complex face embraces all types of climbing from easy scrambling to Grade VI overhangs, from level snow fields to enormous vertical icefalls. The steep, broken bands of rock are a problem as are the violent storms that brew up without warning, but the sandstone girdle in the central section of the face offers really enjoyable climbing, as does the steep summit icefield of the direct route.

The summit itself, the highest in the Andes, is easily reached by its gentle ordinary route from the North and so, for many extreme climbers, the mountain holds no particular allure despite its height above sea level. But to climb the South Face is a different proposition altogether; for the modern top climber it represents an adventure, a mountaineering achievement, and an experience worthy of profound respect.

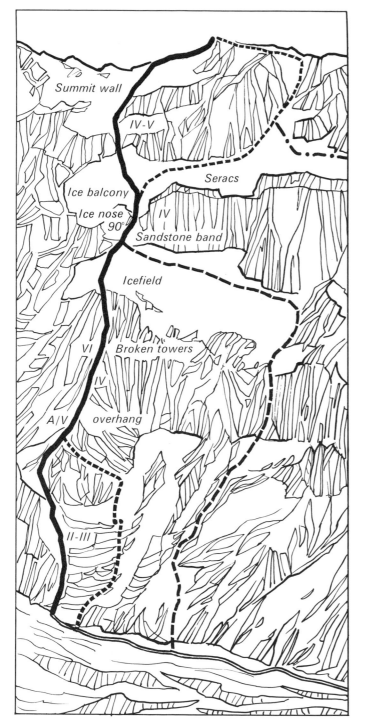

Aconcagua – South Face, Direttissima

The direct South Face Route on Aconcagua Main Summit embraces all stages of climbing.

Summit height: 6,959 m.

Face height: ca. 3,000 m (between 4,000 and 6,959 m).

Difficulties: I–VI, very broken, ice climbing up to 90°.

Duration: After a 2–3 week acclimatisation period, 2–4 days.

Necessary equipment: Crampons, ice axe, short axe, long rock and ice pegs (screws), bivouac tent, down sleeping bag, storm goggles, fixed rope.

Starting point: Plaza de Francia or other places on the left bank of the upper Horcones Glacier (ca. 4,100 m), reached from Puente del Inca (Argentina) via Confluencia in 10–12 hours.

Outline of Route: The strongly-defined buttress in the lower section of the face leads in a straight line to the great glacier basin at two-thirds height. From there a gentle left-hand curve to the summit.

Tips: It is prudent to prepare the first buttress with fixed ropes so that a retreat is always open in the event of a break in the weather.

Good campsites or bivouac possibilities can be found in the gullies above the great, broken buttress and on the great snowfield beneath the summit wall. The remains of old fixed ropes should not be used.

From a safety angle, the only feasible route to the main summit is the central buttress. On the summit wall the South Tyrolean route is preferable to the French route because it is shorter and doesn't present any appreciably greater difficulties.

Aconcagua South Face, seen from the Southwest. ▷

The History

On 14 January 1897 the great Swiss guide, Matthias Zurbriggen, became the first man to stand on the summit of Aconcagua (having already led ascents in the Himalaya and in New Zealand). His client, E. Fitzgerald (English), had succumbed to altitude sickness about 600 metres from the top but had allowed Zurbriggen to carry on alone. So the conquest of the highest Andean summit, first seriously attempted by the German scholar, Dr Paul Gussfeldt, was achieved before the turn of the century.

For a time no-one thought to find other routes on Aconcagua. The ordinary route was repeated and soon claimed its first victim. For many Alpine climbers the violent storms, the altitude and the enormous scale of such a mountain, presented unaccustomed problems, and they needed first to acquire the practical experience to learn to cope with them. Then in 1934 — when it will be remembered that in the Alps the fierce competition for the last great Alpine North Faces was

Dead mule beside the track to Aconcagua.

in full swing — a Polish group climbed Aconcagua from the East and opened up what is perhaps even today the ideal route on the mountain.

But the South Face, which from summit to glacier falls plumb 3,000 metres, was universally considered to be unclimbable. Faces as difficult and as steep were indeed being climbed in the Alps with the conquest of the Matterhorn North Face and the Eigerwand, but only in the Alps. The Eigerwand at that time represented the ultimate possible Big Wall, taking all factors into account — height, difficulty, danger.

And for as long as the Eiger North Face remained the touchstone for the best and most experienced Alpine climbers, Aconcagua's South Face — one and a half times as high again — could not be climbed. Moreover, the Aconcagua face rises to a height of almost 7,000 metres, a height at which the thin air makes itself felt. But even then it could have been foreseen that, in the same way as in the Alps where ambitious objectives have unleashed the powers to accomplish them, so, sooner or later, the precipitous flanks of the seven- and eight-thousand metre peaks would one day be climbed.

Soon after the Second World War the time came when all the eight-thousanders of the Himalaya and Karakorum began to be attempted, firstly by their normal routes, the Big Walls remaining unnoticed. Louis Lachenal — who with Lionel Terray had made the second ascent of the Eiger North Face — succeeded in 1950 in climbing Annapurna summit with Maurice Herzog — this was the first eight-thousander to be scaled. In 1953 Sir Edmund Hillary and Sherpa Tensing Norkay stood on top of Everest and a few weeks later, Hermann Buhl on Nanga Parbat. How long now before the best climbers would have collected sufficient high altitude experience, before the young laid siege on the Big Walls of the highest mountains, before the competition for the Big Walls

The French climbers who succeeded in making the first ascent of Aconcagua South Face in 1954 during bad storms, didn't care to descend via the Ice Nose (right). It is located 2,000 metres above the foot of the face, about 1,000 metres from the summit.

which had already died down in the Alps would be revived in the Andes and Himalaya?

Aconcagua's giant South Face was recognised as a potential mountaineering problem by Lionel Terry and Guido Magnone in 1952. It was first climbed in 1954 after weeks of preparation and under dramatic conditions. A little group of French Alpinists under the leadership of René Ferlet set about to confirm Terray's judgement. To avoid the danger of falling ice on the great, broken wall at the start of the climb, the French chose to follow the line of a pronounced pillar in the central section of the face. It was very difficult and it was necessary to fix ropes for protection, but they accomplished it and went on to overcome the icefields above, the sandstone girdle in the middle of the face, the ice bulge and the exit ramps in Alpine style. Their final assault on the face took seven days. A storm near the summit nearly spelt disaster. The 6-man team — Lucian Bérardini, Edmond Denis, Pierre Lesueur, Robert Paragot, Guy Poulet and Adrien Dagory — put their every effort into struggling through to the summit and succeeded despite exhaustion and bad frostbite. The highest face of the Americas, the Eigerwand of the Andes as it has also been called, was climbed.

The route taken in 1966 by two Argentinians, Georg Aikes and Omar Pellegrini, took a line diagonally across the right hand section of the face, but though it joined the exit ramp of the French route, it remained only a secondary South Face ascent since it avoided the central section of the face entirely.

Also in 1966, during the International Naturfreunde Andean Expedition under Fritz Moravec, a lightning ascent of the South Face was made in which the lower section of the climb was a new variation that joined the French route below the sandstone girdle. This new route is certainly easier than the French route, but the danger of falling ice is so acute that I could not recommend it.

The South Tyrol Andean Expedition of 1974 opened the direct finish to the summit from the great snowfield, completing the French ideal and the resulting climb provides the 'classic' line on this face. Up till then the face had been repeated by two Japanese and one Spanish expedition, all of whom had elected to follow the French route, but it is reasonable to assume that future parties will now take the South Tyrolean line to Aconcagua's main summit.

Direttissima on Aconcagua

The highest face in the New World
was the goal of the South Tyrol Andean Expedition during 1974. As expedition leader, the adventure that reached its climax on the summit of this Andean giant, began for me with the selection of the team. The previous summer I had climbed with some young climbers from the Bolzano high-level group of the South Tyrol Alpenverein, who had trained under Luis Vonmetz. Together we had made new ascents on the Monte Pelmo, the Marmolata and the Furchetta, and as a result I was convinced that there was sufficient talent in South Tyrol for a serious expedition. Practical experience might be lacking, but that could only be gained by going on an expedition.

I talked over my proposal for an attempt on Aconcagua South Face with a South Tyrol team, with Jörgl Mayr and Jochen Gruber, both of whom were very enthusiastic about the project and we decided there and then to try and make the first ascent of either the South Buttress or the Direttissima to the Main Summit. Konrad Renzler, an experienced climber from the Puster valley, with whom I had made several important climbs in the past, agreed to join us, as did Ernst Pertl, the celebrated cameraman and film-maker, with whom I had also climbed. In Doctor Oswald Ölz, who we nicknamed 'Bulle' (the Bull), we found an experienced expedition doctor who because of his climbing abilities was doubly valuable. Oswald and I had already been together on an expedition before when we went to Manaslu in 1972; I therefore knew every single man on our Aconcagua venture from personal mountain experience and hoped that with this strong group we should be able to succeed.

Ruth Ölz, the wife of our doctor, also came with us, as did my own wife, Uschi — both of whom had had expedition experience. I realised they would not be able to help us on the actual face, although Uschi had climbed Mount Kenya and a six-thousander in the Hindu Kush. They were to look after Base Camp and

cook for us since there are no porters on Aconcagua, let alone Sherpas. We never regretted their inclusion in the party. Since one of the objects of this expedition was to give the two young South Tyrol climbers, Gruber and Mayr, their first opportunity to visit a big mountain, I will let one of them give his impressions of the trip — Jochen Gruber, the son of a farmer, from the Sarntal. In his diary he has recorded in his own words all his hopes and experiences. It is reproduced here together with my own recollections. I have not tried to edit it in any way because from it one can recognise just how Jochen thought and felt. His 'Dreams from the Roof of the New World' are typical of how any young climber might feel.

Three years ago
it was only a dream, two years ago it became hope, then reality.

I have been climbing for five years and during this time I have come to know many mountains, undertaken numerous tours in varying grades, have become intimate with both beauty and danger, have dreamt often of distant mountains.

Finally began what was for me the journey of my dreams, a journey to the highest mountain of the New World. After five hour's approach — as, alone with a heavy pack, I was tramping along the Horcones Glacier and the South Face of Aconcagua growing larger by the minute in front of me — many of my inner hopes were realised. In the evenings in Base Camp after the sun had sunk behind the Col Mirador and darkness was gently creeping over the glacier world, I would dream of the last steps to the summit, of shaking my partner's hand, of the hours on the roof of the New World. Every day I looked upwards to the top of the King of the Andes, thought of the climb up its broken face and of the massive avalanches that sweep down.

I went up that face many times; I have slept in Camp I (5,200 m) which clings like an eagle's nest above a huge precipice; I have struggled to build Camp II above the vertical ice bulge at 6,100 m; I have sought to help where I can, have not shunned effort; and just as the summit was about to be stormed, I have lain at Camp II defeated by the might of the mountain. For me a world was shattered, a dream of the summit gone, fate had played me a cruel trick. As Aconcagua's

The Aconcagua South Face offers the modern climber everything: loose rocks, overhangs, vertical ice bulges and narrow cracks, perpendicular chimneys and seemingly-endless icefields. So much variety cannot be found on any Alpine face.

champion victim of altitude sickness, I had to relinquish my position and climb down to Base Camp.

But men continue to dream, and I continued to dream both of mountains at home and mountains of faraway places, and I hope that one day a dream will again become a reality.

27 December 1973

At 7.30 we are at the Railway Station in Bolzano. Jörg, Ernst and I. The express for Frankfurt departs at 8 o'clock. Our personal baggage is stowed aboard and the great journey begins. At 1900 hours we arrive in Frankfurt.

28 December

9 a.m., Station. A great worry is the luggage we sent ahead by rail. But it has arrived already — except that the aluminium chest with the wireless apparatus and films, a tent and some of the medical stores is missing. There is great excitement, to-ing and fro-ing but the chest remains lost. At 13.00 hours the rest of the luggage is despatched and we finally repair to to the Airport. At 22.00 hours our Aerolineas Argentinas Boeing 707 takes off, 2 hours late, for Madrid, where we touch down. After midnight the big flight over the ocean begins.

29 December

We cruise at 10,000 metres. Far below, the sea and the coast of America. At 13.00 hours Central European Time we land in Brazil, the Boeing is refuelled and at 14.00, the great bird soars again into the sky. One hour's flying and we are in Buenos Aires. It is very warm, 28° and summer. At home it is winter. So we must be far from home. Reinhold is waiting for us at the airport. The luggage is despatched without a hitch. Reinhold has organised a bus and a truck from Mercedes, and we go into the town to a German family who have extended to us their hospitality until the 1st of January. First we have lunch, then we can rest.

30 December

We have erected a big tent in the garden and spent the night there. During the day we stroll through Buenos Aires; take a trip on the underground; it is burning hot; busy metropolitan whirl.

31 December

Reinhold and Uschi are busy taking care of the expedition food supplies. We go swimming, lie torpid in the sun. In the evening the New Year's celebrations start. Argentine wine tastes good to all of us and soon everyone is in good humour.

1 January 1974

Today is my birthday. My head is still growling from last night's festivities. I think of my home and friends and how I would dearly like to share days like this with them. I am amazed how far from home I am. In the afternoon we pack up and get ready for the trip to Mendoza. I write a few cards and a letter to my parents. At 23.00 hours the bus and truck leave Buenos Aires. It is a long journey: 1,100 kilometres.

2 January

The bus rolls through the Argentine Pampas. The sky is still hung with low cloud. There has been one almighty thunderstorm in the night. The journey takes all day. We only stop for breakfast and lunch. At 18.00 hours we reach Mendoza — a town of around 100,000 inhabitants — the last jumping-off place for Aconcagua. We all have to go to the Police

The first bivouac tent of the South Tyrol Andean Expedition pitched snugly in a narrow gully. From here the central section of the face can be reconnoitred; 1,000 metres below lies the glacier.

we reach Puente del Inca, the last settlement, really a big military barracks at 2,700 m, where we are to stay. We have a military lunch and in the afternoon take a look at the village and see the local 'sight', a natural bridge after which the place is named. The water has simply carved it out of the rock. The warm spring that used to be a spa, now gushes unchecked over the slopes. The baths are in an indescribable condition, nevertheless we take a splash in the warm, sulphurous water which is about 35 degrees — it should be very healthy. An evening meal that gives us all indigestion and then we sleep in our sleeping bags on the military plank beds.

5 January
Konrad, Jörg and I climb a peak of around 3,900 metres to get acclimatised. We cannot face lunch since we are all still feeling the effects of last night's meal. In the afternoon the loads for the mules are prepared. We have had enough of barrack life and long for peace and for our Base Camp. I have to resist the evening meal also — it is simply too fatty for our taste. In the evening the film 'Somewhere in Tibet' is showing but every five minutes the film tears and so the performance lasts four hours. The soldiers don't make much fuss about it, probably they're used to it.

6 January
Today we want to be in Base Camp. The loads are ready and waiting but the mules must first be caught. It's a slow process, the mules are obstinate and keep tossing off their loads. Several pieces have to be loaded three or four times. Uschi, Ruth and Oswald set off at 8 o'clock and Jörg, Konrad and Ernst get going at 10 o'clock.

Clouds of dust whirled up

as the first beast was led out into the open. It was late morning and the main body of our expedition had already left Puente del Inca some hours before to find a suitable campsite. Now it seemed that the mules allocated us the day before by the Commandant, were not any good. Some needed to be shod before starting, others were incapable of any effort. I was furious and tried to make it clear to the soldiers that we had to get up to the others whatever the cost since we couldn't leave them without sleeping bags and tents. Jochen,

Department. Particulars are taken down to the smallest detail but we can go on tomorrow. The Commissioner of Police invites us to supper and we have a sumptious meal: Asadao, an Argentinian meat dish — goat on a spit — and wine in plenty. The cleanest police school is put at our disposal and we can recover from the fatigue of the journey.

3 January
At 7 a.m. we are back at the Police Station — names, addresses, parents, brothers and sisters, single or married, blood group, passport photos, fingerprints etc. It goes on till noon! After lunch we go to the Board of Public Health where we stay till 15.00 hours. We send the bulk of the expedition greetings cards and at 17.30 we receive our permit for Aconcagua. After a few difficulties with the chauffeur, at 18.00 hours we get on our way in the direction of Puenta del Inca. 20.00 hours we reach Usaplata and there we spend the night in a pleasant hotel.

4 January
We sleep late, and at 10 o'clock continue our way. It reminds me of the Wild West — desert country with deeply-etched river beds, rough roads, dust and wind. At 12 o'clock

The steep ice on Aconcagua was pitted by the heat of the sun providing holds; but the high altitude and the remoteness posed problems.

who from his military service had acquired some knowledge of mules, helped by saddling and loading up. Meanwhile I pursued the Barracks Commander in the hopes of expediting our departure by my persuasion.

The advance party must have reached Confluencia in the meantime, it would have been impossible to call them back now. We therefore had to get up. The soldiers were taking visible pains but the animals were headstrong; they would lie down, throw off their loads, and not once but again and again. Suddenly there was a shouting and commotion, we hardly had time to jump aside, the mules had broken out of their compound — a two metre high stone wall — and were trotting off down the valley, leaving a long trail of dust behind them.

The sight of the disappearing herd was fine, but it brought new difficulties for us; three loads were left behind. We had to make an immediate decision. Jochem would stay behind to supervise the transport of the missing loads the next day; I would set off with three soldiers, nine transport animals and three riding mules to reach the main camp that same evening.

Each Arriero (muleteer) now took charge of three mules, one behind the other, tying the first to his own *mula,* swung himself into the saddle and goaded his beast. I hurried off in front first of all, then behind in order to photograph.

In single file

the heavily-laden animals toiled up the valley. The slopes to the left and right of the hummocky valley floor were arid and barren, of a rust-brown colour. The mountains were bathed in glaring sunlight, there was no mist. The *mulas* trotted along almost soundlessly, seen against the smooth arc of deep blue sky,

their coats seemed to shine. Their tiny hooves rumbled softly and evenly over the stony path and threw up little clouds of dust. We crossed a roaring stream and climbed the very steep slope the other side. I kept going out in front, feeling dry and dusty in the light wind that blew off the mountain, but excited at the prospect of climbing Aconcagua. It was not easy to keep down to the pace of the pack animals.

In Confluencia Ernst, Konrad and Jörgl were waiting for us. Together we set off again behind the mules, but one of the groups of mules slipped and fell a short way, and it took hours before we got all the animals back onto their legs again.

In the late evening we slowly trickled into Base Camp which Dr Ölz and our wives — fit from the march — had selected in a little hollow. The mules, once unloaded, trotted back down the valley the same night with their *arrieros,* fortified by a hearty swig of whisky.

71

When we awoke the next morning, the sun was shining, the wind whistling, and above our heads towered the 3,000 metre high Aconcagua Face, down which avalanches constantly thundered. We moved our campsite because a storm in the night had torn our mess tent, and waited for Jochen who should arrive any moment.

6 January
At 12.30 the first caravan at last gets away. One rider with three heavily-laden mulas. The second caravan again drops its load and the saddling has to start over again. At last at 13.30 the second caravan sets off. I must stay behind since we are short of a mule, I shall come on tomorrow with the last pack animal. Now begins the difficult part of the exercise — to persuade the Commandant to put another mule at my disposal. He has promised before but soon forgotten all about it. The mules are let out to run, the prospect for tomorrow looks black to me. With my scanty vocabulary — a bit of Italian, some English and some Spanish — it must have been a dreadful mixture — I try everything I can in order to be able to reach Base Camp the next day with the last of the luggage. But it all seems to be going wrong. One cannot believe anyone here, everyone makes promises but no-one keeps them. My stomach is still feeling outraged, I cannot eat all day. I feel quite alone here in these barracks, no-one understands German so I can't have a chat with anyone. The time passes uncommonly slowly. I try and talk to the soldiers, my knowledge of Spanish improves noticeably.

7 January
I get up at 7.00, go straight to the mule sheds, but what I had yesterday feared is today confirmed. No mules anywhere, near or far. Somewhat angry, I go to the Commandant and ask him what has happened to his promise. 'Non tengo Mulas, todas cansado' he replies — he doesn't have any mules, they're all tired. After a lot of humming and ha-ing he promises to bring the luggage up the next morning to the old French campsite. I can therefore go up today. Towards 10 o'clock I get away, my rucksack weighing about 12 kgs. I plod steadily across the dry plain towards Aconcagua South Face. On the way I meet an Argentinian Expedition who want to climb the normal route. Their leader is an Italian, Ernesto

Colombero. He is very friendly, gives me a drink and a map to help me find my way. I meet another Italian. He tells me that he is with a Mexican expedition attempting the ordinary route, but one of the Mexicans had been taken ill with altitude sickness and he had accompanied him back to the Plaza de Mulas before returning to his expedition. I say goodbye to Lino, the second Italian, and continue on my way. I make slow progress, the rucksack is cutting into my shoulders. I reach Confluencia — to the left is the way to the Plaza de Mulas, to the right Plaza de Francia. A clear little stream flows through a deep gorge, I drink, rest awhile, then march on. The sun burns down pitilessly, I am alone in this wilderness. I haven't eaten for three days and I'm feeling very empty. I have hardly any strength left and struggle on over heaps of scree and moraine. Aconcagua is still a long way off. I come to a glacier lake, the water is thick and milky, but I am uncomfortably thirsty. I drink although perhaps I shouldn't. My feet burn so I cool them off in the water too. Then I put my boots back on, swing up my rucksack onto my sore shoulders again, I must get on. It is 15.00 hours, I have been five hours so far, the mules usually take seven to reach Base Camp, therefore I still have some three or four hours of walking in front of me.

I continue my solitary way, feeling abandoned. I think of everyone back home. I keep seeing the southern side of Aconcagua, it doesn't look very welcoming. My palate is dry again, my lips chapped. I look for a stream, the water is dirty, brown as coffee. I stoop down, let some of the water flow into my cupped hand, take a little sip but it is impossible to drink. It doesn't matter if there are more streams, if they are like this I shan't drink. I force myself to go on. My steps are getting slower. I reach the top of another moraine hill and can see the foot of the southern buttress. Somewhere there must be the tents, but I can't pick them out. Slowly I toil on. A clear brook again — water — I lunge for it. Then I hear a voice just above me. It is Reinhold. This must be the Base Camp. I take a rest then help with shifting the tents out of the wind, a tent has already been torn to pieces in a storm. At 19.00 hours we have our evening meal, my stomach is back in order. Soon afterwards we crawl into our tents and I certainly sleep well.

8 January
We emerge from the tents at 9 o'clock. It is a beautiful day. Breakfast and immediately afterwards Reinhold and Oswald

take themselves off to the foot of the buttress to look at the situation. Konrad, Jörg and I climb up the left moraine to study the face. We can see how from the great bulge in the middle of the face, great chunks of ice keep breaking off and plunging down into the depths with a mighty roar. They don't seem to fall directly onto the buttress but we cannot be sure. We go back to Base Camp. At 15.00 hours the mules arrive so the Commandant has kept his word. We spend the rest of the day erecting the camp and after our evening meal all disappear into our tents. A cold wind continues to blow. The face keeps sending its greetings of ice and stones, yet it is peaceful here at 4,100 metres. Slowly it gets dark and soon a deep sleep engulfs me.

9 January

We have slept our fill. The weather is windy. The usual morning wash in cold glacier water soon has us wide-awake. Konrad and Jörg will try the start of the buttress today. Ernst goes along with the film camera. I stay in camp, tidy the tent, put up the flysheet and so the afternoon passes. The weather seems to be getting worse. I keep looking at the glacier with the field glasses. Jörg and Konrad have disappeared from view. Towards 14.00 hours, I see Ernst coming back down the glacier. Of Jörg and Konrad there is still no sign. 16.00 hours and still nothing. 17.00 hours still the same. Reinhold and I pack the rucksacks, we will both go and look, perhaps something has happened. Bulle prepares the First Aid things — he is still unwell and follows us slowly. It is 17.30 when Reinhold and I set off. We hurry up the dead glacier. Still no trace. We are worried, something really might have happened. Then at the very end of the glacier our two missing persons come into sight, safe and sound. They have been up on the lefthand moraine to get a better view of the face; the climb over the loose debris had become very tiresome and so made them late. We are happy that everything has turned out well. At 19.00 hours we get back to camp together, have an evening meal and tea, then slide into our tents. The top of Aconcagua is muffled in cloud, a cold wind sweeps over the glacier. I wonder what it's like in South Tyrol now. Cold? Snow? I feel so cut off from my everyday world.

10 January

Early at 7.00, Konrad wakes me. Get dressed, breakfast. Today we want to make a start on the face. Reinhold and I go ahead with about 100 metres of rope, pegs, karabiners,

crampons and axe. Jörg and Konrad follow with more equipment. At 8.45 we leave Base Camp. At 9 o'clock we reach the avalance cone at the foot of the face, which spews onto a steep scree slope. We climb through the loose rocks, resting periodically, looking back. Jörg and Konrad have reached the outer edge of the glacier, they are resting too. We approach the ice towers that completely fill the upper part of the gully. Wearily we work our way round them and reach the first platform. In the same way we continue to the second icefield — ice towers and more ice towers. At 12 o'clock we come to a narrow ridge, a curving ledge leads up over it to the next ice field. Here the seracs are even bigger and deep crevasses often bar the way. We toil upwards, the icefield seems to go on for ever. It is almost impossible to come this way with the loads. We resolve therefore to give up this route, the South Buttress has won again. We turn back. Below the ridge we meet Jörg and Konrad, they're also very tired. Together we climb down, leaving the equipment at the start of the French Route, which will be our next objective. At 8.00 hours we arrive back in Base Camp. Uschi and Ruth have cooked; we are very hungry and thirsty. Soon the sun goes down and we retire to our tents. I can't get to sleep for a long time and play with the idea of the South Buttress, the French Route, the Summit. How will it go?

11 January

Today is rest day. We sleep till 10. The weather is fine in the morning but there is a cold wind. After breakfast we set up a new food store. Ernst is busy with the film. At 13.00 hours we have lunch: lentils and bacon. In the afternoon we talk, discuss things. Bulle is still ill for the third day. The summit of Aconcagua is hidden in cloud and slowly it becomes evening. My thoughts are again high on the summit wall — as well as far away back home.

12 January

At 6.30 I wake up. It is a wonderful morning. Aconcagua is shining in the morning sun. Breakfast and at 7.30 we set off. Reinhold and I go first, Konrad, Jörg and Ernst coming behind with all the gear. At 8 o'clock we reach the dump at the foot of the face, pick up our rope, helmets, axes and pegs, and launch ourselves onto the French Route. In the lower section we can climb unroped without much difficulty. Around 4,400 metres it gets a bit more difficult and we begin to fix ropes. Jörg and Konrad are still a long way down.

Soon we come upon the first camp of the Argentinians who had been the last to climb the face before us. Tentpoles, boots, gas canisters lay about. Reinhold goes on and soon reaches the first steep step upon which the remains of a ladder belonging to an earlier expedition, are hanging. The ladder's ropes are chafed through, they need to be repaired. Now Konrad and Jörg arrive bringing new gear. We climb higher, fixing ropes for a further 80 metres. Following up the fixed ropes, I take more rope and pegs up to Reinhold, which Jörg and Konrad pass me. I belay Reinhold a bit further till he reaches the end of the rope. We leave everything we don't need on the face and rope down. At 17.00 hours we arrive back in Base Camp. Food and drink. Finally we prepare the rope ready for tomorrow. Everyone gets about 60 metres. Towards 20.00 hours I sit in my tent and write my diary, thinking of the day ahead.

13 January

When I first wake up it is 8 o'clock. I peep out of the tent and see Konrad down by the kitchen. The weather, however, seems to be getting worse, another huge avalanche is coming down the face. 'We won't be climbing today' Reinhold says so I go back to sleep till 10 o'clock. Then I edge out of the tent, pulling on my down jacket. It is noticeably colder. I go for my breakfast. At noon everyone is awake and Uschi and Ruth begin to cook. At 13.00 we eat. Afterwards Konrad, Jörg and I take the ropes up to the Argentinian camp. Ernst hauls gear up to the Face Depot. I tie my 60 metres of rope, 3 snow pegs, Karabiners and pitons onto a pack frame and I will pick up Reinhold's crampons at the face depot. A 220 metre rope is already there which I am to pick up in case we need to renew the route to the Argentinian camp. Soon I catch up with Konrad and Jörg who are taking a short cut to the start. Although my load is cutting into my shoulders uncomfortably, I have no difficulty keeping up with the others for I am in fine form. In 2½ hours I have reached the depot at 4,400 m, and soon the other two catch up. Together we climb down. I keep looking down. Everything is so empty and deserted. All sorts of thoughts come into my head. How lovely it is back home, for instance, but also — how beautiful it is here too.

14 January

As usual we scramble out of our tents at 8 o'clock. Splendid weather welcomes us. I look up the face, the lower section is still in shadow. After breakfast I go off with Reinhold. Today we want to prepare the route as far as the great icefield. At 11 o'clock we reach the Argentinian Camp, pick up rope and pegs and go on up, up the fixed ropes. Jumar clamps make the climbing easier and in an hour we reach the upper end of the fixed ropes. Reinhold ties on and begins to climb with me belaying him. It doesn't take long to anchor another 100 metres of rope, and so it goes, higher and higher. Konrad, Bulle and Jörg bring reinforcements. Soon we reach an 80-metre vertical rock band that links us with the great icefield. After some hard work Reinhold overcomes even this obstacle and finds a place for Camp 1. Together we let ourselves down the fixed ropes, an easy and fast descent. In Base Camp Uschi and Ruth are waiting with tea and later give us our evening meal. As soon as the sun goes down it grows cold. We go into the tents. The day was strenuous but we have brought our goal one step nearer.

15 January

It is a rest day for me today but when I wake up at 9 o'clock, I rouse Jörg and tell him he should take the tent up to Camp I with Konrad. They go off at 10 o'clock with heavy packs. A storm tent, stores, sleeping bags and mats have gone with them. They should get up to Camp I and spend the first night at 5,200 m. Today we are visited by an American expedition. They want to take a look at the South Face, then go on to do the ordinary route. We chat, now and then I watch Jörg and Konrad with the telescope. The day passes slowly and towards 16.00 hours we seen Konrad climbing the difficult section immediately below Camp I. Once I have got my rucksack ready for the next day, I crawl into my tent — I have it to myself today. Far away from any habitation with the huge mass of Aconcagua looming overhead, I feel overwhelmed by the distance from home and friends, yet I am glad to be here. This peace — no rush, no hassle — it is another world, another life, and yet so near. A few hours could take me back to civilisation — and home. I sit for a long time in front of the tent whilst the shadows climb gently higher, up from the glacier. Soon they will envelop me too and it will get very cold.

16 January

Today should be another really active day. Reinhold and I want to relieve Jörg and Konrad in order to push on across the icefield the following day to the next rock band. Ernst goes up

with us to film us at work. Bulle belays him on the difficult stretches. With heavy rucksacks we climb over the known route carrying a lot of material for Camp I. Jörg and Konrad climb down with Ernst and Bulle; Reinhold and I settle into the airy camp at 16.30. We brew tea, eat zwieback and cheese. The little perlon tent flutters madly in the terrific gusts of wind, although we are fairly well protected. We talk a while and soon creep into our sacks. At 21.00 hours we signal with the handlamp down to Base Camp, but there is no reply.

17 January
A thunderous cracking and crashing rips me from my sleep; an avalanche is coming down to the left of the buttress. A glance at my watch shows it is 8 o'clock. The sun shines cheerfully into our little nest. We make tea and have breakfast, then set to work. The customary wash is dispensed with. Our rucksacks are heavy with 150 metres of rope, a bundle of ice pegs, ice screws and snow pegs, as well as crampons and personal gear. We have to be prepared for the Viento blanco, the White Wind, notorious for its cold. Up through icy gullies and over quantities of broken rock; we come to the

relics of an old Japanese camp. All that remains of the tent are tattered shreds, witness to the ferocity of the Viento blanco, boots are frozen into the ice, tent poles, a book and all sorts of bits and pieces. We reach the top of the buttress, buckle on our crampons and trudge up the seemingly endless icefield. At 11 o'clock we reach the rock band, far bigger than we had expected. It rises steeply above us, almost vertically like a Dolomite wall — good rock awaits us. Reinhold climbs up, putting in pegs, anchoring the rope, and I follow on the fixed rope. In three hours we have this obstacle behind us and for as long as the rope lasts, Reinhold climbs the vertical icefall above, which towers some 100 metres over us. He gets in a good ice screw and comes back down. We descend to Camp I where we meet Bulle, who has brought up a second tent for Camp II as well as ropes and provisions. Bulle wants to stay in Camp I and work on the ice bulge with Reinhold the next day, so after a short rest I leave Camp I and an hour and a half later reach Base Camp. I have to pass on the plan of campaign for tomorrow and greetings from Reinhold and Bulle to their wives. After the meal we turn in. Soon a bad thunderstorm blows up and it begins to snow. Spooky flashes of lightning, growls of thunder, the

tents flap in the wind. The sleet rattles against the roof of the tent. Gradually sleep overpowers me

18 January

The storm is over, our Base Camp wears a wintry guise. Luckily the tents have stood up to it all and everything has stayed dry. I carefully peel myself out of my sleeping bag and venture out into the cold. Jörg and Konrad are getting equipment together for their climb. Soon the sun comes up and in the wink of an eye, everything changes completely. I can see Jörg and Konrad climbing up the face, Reinhold and Bulle at work on the ice bulge. In the afternoon it starts to snow again and a bit later I see four figures emerging from the mist, coming down the fixed ropes. At 19.00 hours everyone is back in Base. It's still snowing on the face. After supper we discuss the position.

19 January

Today the weather is wonderful. Whilst we are chatting over breakfast, I am dreaming about a possible summit bid, and 10 minutes later Reinhold says Jörg and I should go up to Camp I today, spend the night there and climb on the next morning. He will then follow. It is with some emotion that I pack my rucksack, put on my leather breeches, carefully do up my triple boots. We have been a long time sweating and straining on this face — will we be rewarded with the summit? Anxiously I wonder if I'll get back to Base Camp safely, if I'll ever see my home and loved ones again? At 14.00 hours Jörg and I start off, the rucksacks are astonishingly heavy and cumbersome — there is so much we need to take up in the way of stores and equipment. At 18.30 we reach Camp I, brew tea and have some fish, sausage and crispbread. Whilst we are getting the tents organised, the two sleeping mats for Camp II slip away and whistle off into space — annoyed at the loss, I slide into my sleeping bag. It will soon be tomorrow.

20 January

Something wet touches my face and gives me quite a shock. It is the wall of the tent on which the condensation has built up. A glance at the time — 8 o'clock. A bit sleepy I start brewing tea. Soon Jörg is awake and we tackle breakfast. In the morning sun we film Camp I with a small camera that Ernst has given me to take on the summit bid. We pack the

View from second bivouac on Aconcagua at 6,150 m, towards the South Summit.

rucksacks with all the things necessary for Camp II and at 9 o'clock we move off. Reinhold emerges through a gap, he is coming straight up from Base; we wait for him at the start of the ice field. Together we climb higher, stopping for rests, photographing and slowly gaining height. I feel in good form even though the rucksack is cutting into me. At 15.00 hours Reinhold and I reach the ice bulge of which another 80 metres or so still need roping up. Reinhold wrestles with the almost vertical ice and at 16.00 hours we finally both step out onto the snow plateau above the ice cliff. I have to go back some 250 metres to fetch the tent that we left down on the rock band. Slowly I toil back up through the vertical rock and ice zone and in an hour, get back to where I left my rucksack on the plateau. Reinhold and Jörg have already disappeared behind a promentary; I snatch up the rucksack, tie on the tent and follow their tracks up to the camp site. In the last of the evening sunshine we reach Camp II at a height of about 6,150 m. When the sun goes down it gets very cold and we take refuge in the tent. The humming of the cooker and the smell of tea revive us. It gets quiet in the tent, but a stabbing pain in my tooth keeps jerking me out of my doze.

21 January

The rime that has built up inside the tent during the night, gradually evaporates. Outside the sun is shining. Reinhold cooks tea and soup. I have no appetite today, only thirst. Towards midday Jörg climbs down to wait for Bulle and Konrad at the beginning of the plateau. Reinhold and I go on to reconnoitre the exit rocks. We only have some 20 metres of rope and soon there is nothing for it but wait for the new supplies to come up. We have an idea of the difficulties on the summit wall and turn back to Camp II. Towards 18.00 hours we are joined by Bulle and Konrad. The second tent is erected, tea brewed and a meal eaten. Bulle gives me some pain-killing tablets. The night draws in, eerily. For me it is a miserable night. My head throbs, my tooth aches and towards morning I lie awake, thirsty and wretched. It gradually dawns on me that my dreams of reaching the summit will never materialise. The hours drag by. Suddenly a violent storm blows up, threatening to rip the tent to pieces. We hang on to it from the inside; the inferno lasts an hour.

22 January

The uproar is over, peace again prevails on our plateau. I have to keep pulling myself together to hear what the others are saying, my brain seems to have seized up. For me there is only one thing that matters now: to get back to Base Camp. At 11 a.m. I have my things together, am equipped with axe and crampons, but not for a summit climb, for a bitter descent. Bulle and Jörg come with me. I have the greatest difficulty keeping on my feet. I look up at the summit of 'my' mountain, for which I have devoted so much time and energy. It seems so near and at the same time unutterably far. A few parting words and I stagger off, belayed by Bulle. Once down the bulge, Jörg goes back up to Camp II and Bulle escorts me down alone. It is only with the utmost effort that I can force myself down. Bulle is touchingly sympathetic, and so we make our laborious way, metre by metre back down the mountain. Far below we can see a little yellow spot, Base Camp. After a 7-hour struggle we reach the foot of the face. Now we only have to negotiate the 200 metres down the glacier to camp. Ernst comes up to meet us, takes my rucksack, gives me tea and after another weary hour we reach camp. Soon I am in my sleeping bag, in our doctor's hands, and I fall into a deep sleep.

Next day, a crucial decision had to be taken — we all knew that, and I more than any, for I had seen the hopes of a summit success diminish minute by minute over the last 24 hours. I resolved that the next morning Jörgl and I would venture a lightning attempt on the summit, not forgetting that we would both have to climb down the South Face afterwards. Bulle had of course taken some of the rope to belay Jochen down the ice bulge, so any rope we needed for the summit bid, we must bring back to Camp II with us for the retreat down the face with Konrad.

Early the next morning, 23 January, Jörgl (who is often mistaken for the pop-singer, Heino) and I set off over the snow slopes and vertical ice sections towards the rock band on the summit wall, which had already caused us some head-scratching on the reconnaissance. The rock is very loose and poorly-stratified, and I took over the lead from Jörgl at this stage. But we only made slow progress, partly because we were belaying one another and partly because the altitude was increasingly affecting Jörgl.

At the top of the rock barrier, some 6,400 metres above sea-level, we reviewed our position and eventually decided that I should climb on to the summit alone, since as a roped party we only had the slimmest chance of getting there the same day. It had already taken us more than four hours to cover the first 400 metres, and as there were still some 600 between us and the summit, we really had no other choice. This was the simple compromise solution. In his exhausted state, Jörgl readily agreed to the plan and promised to wait for me on a rock ledge. I assured him I would be back in four or five hours. He tied himself on, keeping the rope, and I climbed on alone.

I travelled very fast because if I wanted to keep my promise and not endanger my companions, I needed to make at least 200 metres of height an hour. I knew I could do it as I had often climbed as fast at such altitudes, but I must allow for unexpected difficulties.

23 January

As I awake the sun is already shining outside. Everything that has happened comes back to me like a bad dream. I feel better. We keep looking up to the top of the face. Towards noon we spy a black dot moving through the icefield towards the summit. It must be Reinhold. He moves upwards at a steady pace. Later we see another dot, following the first. Jörgl or Konrad? But this dot soon turns back.

Through the mist

which now blanketed everything, I suddenly made out the outline of Jörgl, who seemed to be following me. Obviously he was feeling a bit better and was now attempting to catch up.

I climbed a steep icefield, covered with a thin spongy crust, and would have been happier if I were belayed. Over me there was a bulge in the face and the Guanaco Ridge was hidden from view.

I was worried for Jörgl. He might take on too much, or in his weakened state, slip and fall. I therefore called down to him to go back to his platform and wait there as we had agreed. I was relieved to see him turn back. Were he to have gone further, I would have had no choice but to climb back down to him and forego the lightning dash to the summit. I could not let him climb this steep terrain unbelayed, and as a roped party we would be too slow, as we were before. On top of this, the weather was worsening — Jörgl wears glasses — so there was no other option. I would dearly have liked to stand on the summit of Aconcagua with him, or indeed with one of the others, but I had to go on alone, very fast so that we could get down the same day, if we were not to surrender success altogether. Within a few days our expedition would be going back to Europe, our holiday was coming to an end.

With a watch and an altimeter

I climbed upwards, at the same time thinking about our return march, how we must get off soon to arrive in Mendoza in good time; and I thought of our comrades back in Base Camp. The higher I climbed, the more steps I could take before taking a rest, propped on my ice axe. I had found my rhythm and was covering more than 200 metres of height in the hour.

23 January, 14.00 hours

I long to be up on the face. Only now is it properly coming home to me that my long-cherished hopes have come to naught. In the afternoon clouds settle around the face, we can no longer follow what is happening up there.

The storm

caught me so sharply in the face as I looked over the Guanaco Ridge that it felt as if my head would be wrenched off. I immediately withdrew and climbed back over broken rocks to a position on a narrow ledge on the South Face. There was practically no wind at all here, threads of cloud were whisked over the knife-edged ridge and the roaring of the wind overhead was louder than ocean rollers.

On my little sheltered perch high on the uppermost crags, I took off my rucksack, pulled out my over-trousers and a second anorak and put them both on. Then over my fur cap I wore a storm helmet, exchanged my sunglasses for some ski goggles that covered my face, and put on my down mittens. 'Viento blanco, I said half-aloud, 'We'll see about Viento blanco'. As I set off again I thought of this cold wind that freezes everything in its path — one reads about it in all the accounts of Aconcagua and indeed I had dreaded this wind far more than all the difficulties on the entire face. But I was now only a few metres below the summit and didn't want to give up. Again I ventured onto the ridge linking the South Summit with the Main Summit, and again the storm ate right into my clothes. But now I could bear it. I stood up, faltered for a moment in the

Aconcagua South Face — Grade VI — about 5,000 metres above Sea Level. The Direttissima could only be completed after the difficult passages at the start of the face had been safeguarded with fixed ropes. The retreat was left open in case of bad weather or illness. Pictured here, Oswald Ölz.

force of the blast, and then as I found my balance again. began to climb upwards over the rough blocks. As quickly as was possible at this height, I made for a big rock on the ridge, in order to shelter behind it. Gasping, I reached it and cowered down behind it. I was about halfway between the saddle and the main summit on what is called the Guanaco Ridge. The pointed South Summit lay immediately below me and when I looked back across the inhospitably steep rock and ice of the South Face, which I had just climbed, I didn't care to think about going down again. And yet I had to descend this same face, my companions were waiting for me down there.

It was not quite 3 o'clock, at 5 I must be back with Jörgl. I still needed to hurry for I would soon have to turn back. I straightened up and struggled on, making for another large block on the ridge.

Suddenly, just below me to the left, I noticed a man climbing down a wide gully full of loose stones. He was alone, dressed in a red anorak. With two ski sticks, he prodded his way down the stones interminably slowly. For a few moments I even doubted whether it was a man at all or whether I was being plagued with hallucinations.

The tiny figure

seemed hardly to move perceptibly, yet there was a rhythm to his movement. First he would test the loose ground with his left ski stick, plunge it in, then slowly lift the right and repeat the exercise till both sticks were standing in the loose ground. Only then when the second stick was firmly placed, would he move himself, leaning forward supporting his trunk on the two sticks, he would take a few tiny steps. His knees seemed to give way, his boots merely to brush the rocks beneath him.

Just below the man must be the Canaletta, a nar-

rowing of the normal route, a bottle-neck that has to be crossed on the way to the summit. Far below him I believed I could pick out tents, yellow and red. How small they were, mere specks on a vast, stony hillside. Would the descending climber ever reach them? I had been thinking clearly enough but suddenly I was seized with a feeling of utmost abandonment, seeing this staggering figure heading away from me.

This man didn't belong to our expedition, I didn't even know him. He was on the ordinary route, a different route, going down. But suddenly I had been so pleased to see another human being in these hostile surroundings, that I sought to call after him. He obviously didn't hear me, continued to climb calmly and slowly down on his ski sticks. He left me with the impression of an amputee, using his last ounce of strength to labour on crutches through the sharp rocks. Again I called after him, but again he showed no reaction. For a few moments I was aware of a desire to climb down with him, to accompany him, to assist him, but then I thought of my own comrades waiting below, and climbed on a bit faster.

From block to block, I toiled up through a rocky couloir, having meanwhile left the crest of the ridge itself. About 20 metres below me some rags were fluttering in the wind. It didn't take me long to realise this was the body of a dead climber. He lay with his face towards the valley, just there on the stones as if he had collapsed and not had the strength to pick himself up again.

The dead man seemed at one with the stones,

a red bundle amongst the rocks. Yet my feelings resisted this impression. I just stood there rooted to the spot; I placed my right foot on a rock and rested my right elbow on my knee so that I could hold my head. I was breathing badly. Although my eyes were shut

Dr Oswald Ölz (right) accompanied Jochen Gruber (left) to Base Camp when he was suffering from the effects of altitude. He had to abandon his own hopes of reaching the summit. Although in fine form himself, he put the welfare of his comrades above personal success.

bered that I had heard on the march-in that a Japanese climber had lain dead for a year just under the summit, frozen. Viento blanco, perhaps, I thought — or it might have been exhaustion as well, or altitude sickness. The storm tore at his clothes. I made an effort not to look back at him any more, I tried to forget him. I had to climb down myself this day, I must concentrate.

Suddenly a little to the left I could make out a white cross, about a metre high, made of aluminium and bent by the wind. I was on the summit!

After a short pause

I took off my rucksack and weighted it down with a big stone, so that the storm could not carry it off, and I looked around me. In the North and West the surrounding peaks were clear of cloud, there were wide glaciers, and here and there rocks. Far below on the seemingly endless stonefields of the Northwest Flank, I could again make out the red dots, tents probably. Is that where the man I had seen earlier was heading? To the South thick cloud banners hung from the ridge so that I could not look down at the great glacier plateau where our two tents were standing. After taking a few photographs, I dragged out a little box from under an aluminium shield that lay on the summit, rummaged among all the scraps of paper and little flags left there by my predecessors and read some of the names. Then with stiff fingers I wrote inside an old film carton: 'First direct ascent of Aconcagua South Face by the South Tyrol Andean Expedition 1974, on 23.1.1974' and underneath that I inscribed my name. This piece of card I left with the other documents in the box and put the lid back on, leaving it as I had found it.

We should have been five on the summit at that moment if the bad bout of altitude sickness had not thwarted our plans and hopes.

tight I could still see the dead man in front of me, see how he had been climbing down from the summit, lost his balance, fallen heavily and been unable to get up. He didn't move again. Now the storm tore at his clothes. Although I was in quite good shape myself, strange thoughts pursued me. At such heights a stumble can be fatal. Perhaps he had been a good climber, perhaps he had only wanted to sit down.

I didn't dare sit down now, I had to get on. I climbed steadily but I couldn't shake the image of the dead man from my thoughts. Vaguely now I remem-

Half past four in the afternoon —
high time to start the descent. Once more I turned back to look at the summit. Back at the stones, smooth and grey-brown, heaped, layered, lost for all time. For a short while I too was as distant from all life as these stones, as bereft of desire. I heard only the wind that blew through my head, right into my brain. The stones crunched under my feet but I was not conscious of movement. The clouds swelled over the Guanaco Ridge and I plunged into them until storm and dream were mingled, until I was going along the sharp ridge, timeless, in clouds of stars.

I retraced my steps back along the ridge to the exit down onto the South Face, then clambered carefully down the steep slope. I had trouble finding my tracks because the ice in this upper section was quite blank. Going down, crampons had to be placed even more particularly than coming up. A crevasse required the utmost concentration; further down, the face was covered in snow and the cloud made it even more difficult to find traces of my route.

Jörgl was as pleased to see me as I him when we met up again in the late afternoon where we had parted five hours before. Small powder-snow avalanches poured over us as we abseiled down the lower summit wall, snatching our breath away and giving us no respite. It was snowing and every ten minutes or so the new snow would break away far above us and flow down the cracks and chimneys in little avalanches.

Konrad welcomed us with a mug of hot tea at the camp — more of a bivouac than a camp — and the next day we were able to celebrate our success all together in Base Camp.

23 January, evening
By 18.00 hours I am worn out and ready for bed. I retire into my tent. For a while all manner of thoughts chase round my head, but I soon slip off into a restoring sleep.

24 January
I have slept for a long time. Today I feel as right as rain, well enough to be able to start climbing again. Bulle is regarding the face through the telescope, there is no sign of movement. At last, towards mid-day, three dots can be seen on the ice bulge, they move slowly downwards. All day long I watch what's happening up there. At 16.00 hours Uschi and Bulle go to the foot of the face; Ruth, meanwhile, is preparing a celebration meal. At 19.00 hours we are all together again in Base Camp, safe and sound. Ernst films, beer is drunk and the success toasted. After the good evening meal, we chat a long time and hear of the solo ascent to the summit, of the descent to Camp II, the snowslides, the cold, of success.

Under Ruth and Uschi's tender care
Jochen had visibly recovered. Ernst, who had shot a television film of the expedition for RAI/TV, came out to meet us bearing a clump of saxifrage, a browny-green flower greeting, a token of the ice, sand and wind that had constituted our lives for the past three weeks.

An aluminium cross, distorted by the wind; some scraps of paper in a box — that was the summit of Aconcagua.

25 January

I don't wake until 10.00, crawl slowly out of the tent and go to breakfast. Then I pack my things and at 12 o'clock set off for Puenta del Inca. My job is to organise the mules and send them back to pick up our luggage. Again I leave Base Camp on my own and wander out through the desert-like landscape of the wild Horcones Valley. In 2 hours I reach Confluencia; there I meet the Americans who visited us in Base Camp. We talk awhile, as well as our language difficulties permit. After half an hour I go on, meet the members of an Austrian expedition under Markus Schmuck, who have climbed the ordinary route. With them I reach Puente del Inca at 17.00 hours. That same evening I talk with the Commandant and he promises nine mules for the next day. All OK. That evening there is also a group from Ravensburg staying at the barracks, they have climbed the Polish Route. We chew the fat for a bit before going to sleep. I have to content myself with sleeping on the floor tonight.

26 January

I am woken up by a lot of noise in the room quite early. The Austrians (Schmuck Expedition) are beginning to pack. When peace returns I sleep on till 10 o'clock. I soon realise that there won't be any mules left over for us, and that I will have my hands full trying to sort things out. I spend the whole morning with the officers, deliberating, but nothing comes of it, there isn't a single mule for us. In the afternoon I try again for all my worth. Hopeless, not a mule to be had, near or far. Evening arrives and again I must put up with sleeping on the floor. It doesn't matter any more. I have grown accustomed to a lot of things.

27 January

I get up fairly early and set off towards Punta de Vacas, a village some 40 kilometres away. I am determined to get there as soon as possible. Soon someone gives me a lift, but unfortunately after a few kilometers the vehicle stops and nothing whatever will persuade it to get going again. I march on on foot and finally reach the village at a trot. My luck is no better there, not a mule to be had. There is nothing for it but to turn round and start back again. After about four hours I reach the car that gave me a lift earlier, the breakdown service has arrived. An ancient vehicle is hitched to the four-litre car and together they chug back along the rugged

track until the breakdown truck itself fails. Repairs get under way but the motor stays dead. I set off again on foot. The people in Puente del Inca all know me by now; I am invited to lunch with a railway worker's family. They have a little hut with thick walls and one tiny window. It is very dark inside. Three grubby, sunburnt children run around and regard me with big dark eyes. I am given eggs, home-baked bread and a kind of salad. It tastes good even if its cleanliness may leave something to be desired. My knowledge of Spanish is just sufficient to allow me to talk a little. The people have a great respect for the Sur del Aconcagua, the South Face, and consider me something of a hero to have been on it. I stay with them till quite late in the afternoon. I am hoping someone will arrive from Base Camp in the evening. I even get a bed tonight and just as I drop off at midnight Bulle and Ruth arrive. I tell them the woeful story of the Mulas.

28 January

Today Bulle and I try again to get some mules, but even with two of us it doesn't help. So we decide to bring all the gear down ourselves. Ruth goes on to Mendoza and I set off back to Base Camp. The sun scorches down as I trek along the familiar route for the third time. In Confluencia I meet the mule caravan on its way back to the Plaza de Mulas. Slowly I plod on and come to the little stream with the only drinkable water and quench my thirst. A short while later I meet Reinhold and Uschi. We discuss the position, they go on down, I up. At 19.00 hours I reach Base Camp. The other three are already eating; I tell them of our new plan. But looking at the massive piles of luggage, we don't know how we shall ever shift it all. We get the first loads ready for the next day then go to sleep.

29 January

Up at 7.00, have some soup, then shoulder our rucksacks. Each load weighs about 35 kilos and it is not long before our shoulders become very sore. We struggle glumly downwards — it is a long way down the Horcones Glacier. Soon we meet Bulle, and a little later on, Reinhold. It seems our task will be somewhat easier than we thought; we can dump the loads at Confluencia as some mules will be coming up tomorrow from the Plaza de Mulas. We reach the cluster of low huts at 11 o'clock, take off our packs and rest; then after two hours we climb back up. The heap of baggage is still *formidable. I start piling things onto a packframe: 2 medicine chests, 4 ropes (each 50–80 metres long), my own rucksack weighing some 10 kilos — that makes about 40 kilos altogether. Staggering under the weight, I leave the campsite that has been my home for so long, at 19.00 hours. We haven't got much time as it will soon be night. The trip this morning took three hours. The last rays of sun are already catching the mountain tops and soon it will be dark. We reach Confluencia by the light of our head-torches. We find our way into the little shelter, slip into our sleeping bags and soon fall asleep.*

30 January

The shelter where we are sleeping is so small that I butt my head against the ceiling as I sit up, and reel back as if I've been punched. We share out breakfast — a tin of sardines between three, a piece of bread, some water to drink. Our requirements are modest. Bulle soon shows up, he has spent the night half-way down. Reinhold and Ernst come in at 10 o'clock. All the loads are here. We look along the track towards Plaza de Mulas, but there are no mules in sight yet. A little after 10, I go off to waylay the truck that should be meeting us at 12. On the track I meet a group of Austrians who are coming to do the ordinary route. They are in the same fix as us — no mules. We chat, I learn of the death of Felix Kuen, we certainly have been cut off from all the news. I get on my way again and at 11 o'clock, reach the road and wait for the truck. No sign of it yet. Slowly I wander down to the Horcones Lake, which is a local beauty spot. Four young Argentinians are already there, cooking sausages. They invite me to share their meal and I gladly accept as I am fairly hungry. Soon the truck comes, but no mules. Reinhold, Konrad and Bulle arrive with their loads; the mules have again left us in the lurch. We all go on to Puenta del Inca and have some lunch. I load my rucksack up with food for Jörg and Ernst who are still at Confluencia, and soon I am marching back up to them in the boiling heat. My sleeping bag is my constant companion, my rucksack my constant affliction. Just as I am crossing a raging stream by a little narrow bridge, far away in the distance, I make out three mules with our luggage. Jörg and Ernst join me and tuck into the provisions I have brought. Together we reach the barracks. After a long shower we feel freshened-up and our worries are all forgotten.

31 January

Today we travel down to Mendoza. At 12 o'clock we are all stowed into the bus and travelling along a dusty road through this 'Wild West' landscape. We are delayed for a few hours when the radiator breaks down. In the late afternoon we reach Mendoza, find the hotel where Konrad, Bulle, Ruth and Uschi are staying. Today we have a real meal again. Konrad, Ernst, Jörg and I then stroll around the town. We don't go to sleep till late.

1 February

The bus is repaired and can go on. Argentine climbers buy — and pilfer— equipment from us. Soon the trading is over. At 14.00 hours we start in the direction of Buenos Aires; the journey takes all night.

2 February

In the first grey light of day we reach Buenos Aires. We buy a few souvenirs and at 14.00 hours all meet up in Eseiza, the airport. Jörg and I are only on the 'wait-list', we may have to fly on later. Reinhold succeeds in booking us onto the same flight as the others. At 17.00 hours the Boeing 707 takes off, stopping at Sao Paulo, Rio de Janeiro and Madrid. Home is not far away now.

3 February

At 13.00 hours Central European Time, we land in Rome. Our luggage is put onto an Alitalia Caravelle and at 18.00 hours we are back in Milan. It is dreadful weather — we have been used to it being summer.

4 February

At 2 o'clock in the morning our train stops in Bolzano. Four bearded figures step out and unload an assortment of baggage. The big adventure is at an end. We are pleased that all went well. This expedition was, for me, a tremendous experience, and I would like to thank all those who, one way or another, made it possible for me to go. Above all, I would like to thank our leader, Reinhold Messner, who organised everything, and naturally all my other team-mates as well. Many thanks for those happy days on Aconcagua!

Lhotse (8,511 m). Its South Face ranks amongst the most difficult in the world. At 3,500 metres it is not so high as the Rupal Face, and less dangerous than the South Face of Dhaulagiri, but steeper and achieving a higher altitude. At eight-and-a-half-thousand metres this vertical face may well be impossible. In places the Lhotse Face even overhangs.

Modern Expeditions

The days when big expeditions were organised or financed nationally, or by clubs, is over. Certainly there are still some expedition 'managers' who, by arranging contracts with the mass-media, by fund-raising or through industrial or political contacts, can get expeditions on their feet and invite top climbers to participate, but nowadays it is much more usual for small groups of friends to plan and set off for some distant mountains in much the same way as they would once have gone to the Western Alps.

Nor does a mammoth expedition have any more chance of success than a small party. And for the individual participant, the financial burden can be equally heavy, if not heavier on a big expedition, since the 'manager' usually requires a hefty contribution from each member of his team, whereas, on a small expedition, because of its lightness, savings can often be made on freight, porterage and organisation costs.

My understanding of a modern expedition is, therefore, one where a group of friends have come together and set themselves the objective of some high or difficult peak amongst the mountains of the world. Obviously considerable preparation is necessary, the acquirement of equipment does cost money, and

not all prospective participants may have sufficient holidays. However, half a dozen friends can take advantage of cheap group air-travel, and there are many worthwhile Big Walls that can be climbed in three or four weeks.

For our Aconcagua South Face expedition, we neither planned years ahead, nor got involved in greetings-card schemes, nor indeed 'begged' in any way. Nor did we require our team members to sign any form of 'contract'. As leader of the expedition, I was of the opinion that a contract could not remove any of the difficulties encountered on an expedition and, moreover, it would represent an interference with the personal liberty of participants. It was left to each individual to put in a proportion of the costs, although I bore a significantly larger share of expedition expenses than the others. Also, everyone was free to give his own account of the experiences after the expedition, as he saw them; there was no 'official-expedition-story-line'.

If an expedition runs smoothly without any friction, there are unlikely to be any seriously different interpretations of events afterwards. But if differences of opinion do emerge, there is nothing an expedition contract could do to remove them. Fundamentally, any argument belongs within the framework of an expedition, and, if suppressed at the time, can get distorted, if not to say falsified, afterwards. It would be quite absurd to instruct a court of law to discover what happened, for instance, just below the summit of Aconcagua South Face. Outsiders cannot establish what happened, nor appreciate the feelings of the people involved, nor really even examine or criticise them.

For these reasons I rejected the idea of any expedition contract, and to this day, I have never regretted my decision. After our return to South Tyrol, Jörg Mayr did in fact tell quite a different story of the summit bid than he had in Argentina; he claimed that I had denied him the opportunity of reaching the summit. This assertion was really the result of pressure from outside — people were constantly harrassing him on how he felt about the subject. But I must take some of the blame myself; maybe I made a mistake in my choice of participants. The moral I draw from all this is that in future I must be more careful when choosing my climbing companions.

Financing the expedition was no real problem in as much as the foreseeable expenses were divided equally between the eight team members. Baron Di Pauli from Kaltern, himself an enthusiastic mountaineer, sent the expedition a generous, unsolicited contribution when he learned of our plans; it was doubly appreciated for not having been requested. Also the headquarters of the South Tyrol Alpenverein grant-aided the two youngest members, Gruber and Mayr. This kind of assistance on the part of an Alpine organisation is, I feel, very significant, because without it many competent climbers in their younger years would have no chance of getting to foreign mountains.

That the expedition in the final analysis cost more than expected, could not have been foreseen, and I as leader took on these extra expenses. I hoped in the course of a year to recoup them through lectures, articles and books.

The leadership of the expedition was mine from the beginning because of my experience, but we all planned and discussed the course of events on the mountain. I don't hold with authoritarian leadership on an expedition, especially if the leader has not been chosen by the team, nor by virtue of his climbing experience, his knowledge and his organisational skills. The responsibility that I, as leader, bore on Aconcagua was to gently direct proceedings and, at the critical moment, to climb to the summit alone.

Kangchenjunga (8,598 m) has no route yet on its North or
Northeastern side. As early as 1929 and 1931, the German, Paul
Bauer, attempted the Spur with his expeditions, but hardly anyone
has considered the Face. Is it too dangerous for an ascent?

Paiju Peak, Biaho Tower and Trango Towers. They stand on the orographic right of the Baltoro Glacier and are composed of firm, rusty-red granite.

Self-fulfilment and Self-healing by Climbing

How many of us suffer in one form or another from the fact that our energies and skills are not being properly utilised. More than three-quarters of all people in the Industrial West, say the statisticians. I don't know. I only know that under-realisation of the bodily and emotional resources promotes a cancer of the soul, an unlived life. There are many ways one can safeguard oneself against this. Climbing Big Walls, for example, is one.

In the Karakorum alone, there are so many Big Walls that one man's climbing life is not time enough to even look at them all, to say nothing of attempting to climb them. The faces of the Trango Towers are more than 2,000 metres high and every bit as steep as the granite bastions of El Capitan; the hidden East Face of Paiju Peak is hung with cascades of ice; and in the Latok Group there are many faces still awaiting discovery.

In Alaska, too — I think of the faces on Lotus Flower Tower alone; in Canada, in the Garhwal, in Sikkim (photo pages 92/93) and Kashmir, there are so many undiscovered Big Walls that the young extreme climber need have no fear. One needs only the idea — and the perserverence to make the idea come true. The North Face of Masherbrum represents a very big problem. To say nothing of the West Face of Gasherbrum, which is both vertical and loose at the same time.

90

Nanga Parbat South Face

The South Face of Nanga Parbat, known also as the Rupal Face, rears 4,500 metres up above the Tap Alpe, and ranks amongst the greatest precipices in the world. It is not as inaccessible as the faces of other eight-thousanders, but its very contrast with the gentle, alpine meadows immediately beneath it, gives it a special fascination.

When A. F. Mummery, and later Willo Welzenbach and Willy Merkl, saw the Rupal Face, they none of them thought it would ever be possible to climb it. Even Hermann Buhl, who having climbed the Walker Spur and the Eigerwand, and for a short time afterwards played with the idea of attempting Aconcagua South Face, considered the South Face of Nanga Parbat to be positively unscalable, after seeing it a few times from the Southeast Flank.

Everyone who has ever stood at the foot of this face, studied it or flown over it, could not help but have been amazed by its sheer size; it has become known as 'the highest rock and ice wall in the world'.

Relatively gentle at its base, the first 2,000 metres of the face are not difficult, but from there it builds up, steeper and steeper, the higher it goes. The route winds up through the buttressed central section of the face and is logical and relatively-well protected. It is a route of spurs, icefields and gulleys that leads out onto the summit of the ninth highest mountain in the world — a challenging prospect for the modern Alpinist.

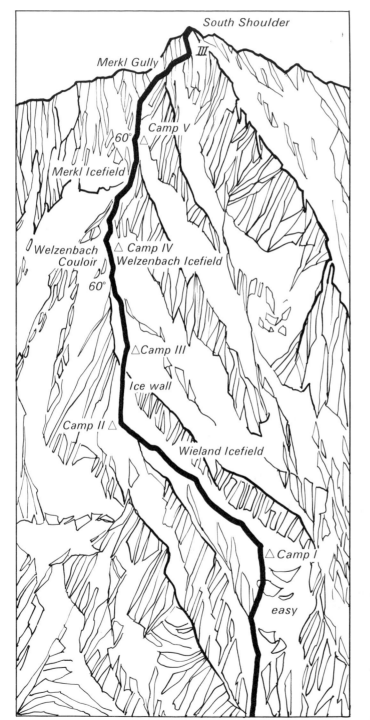

Nanga Parbat — South Face, Central Pillar

The difficulties of the Rupal Flank are mainly ice-climbing difficulties.

Summit height: 8,125 m.

Face height: ca. 4,500 m (between 3,650 and 8,125 m).

Difficulties: II–IV, mostly iced, ice slopes of up to 90°.

Duration: 4–6 weeks preparation and acclimatisation, and a final 5–8 days for the complete climb.

Necessary equipment: Besides the best rock and ice equipment, fixed ropes will also be needed, tents (and accessories), radio apparatus, first class bivouac equipment and medical supplies, to be taken to the highest camp.

Starting point: Tap Alpe (3,560 m). Reached from Gilgit (Pakistan) via Indus, Astor and Rupal Valleys (jeep road and footpath).

Route — Outline: The route mainly keeps to the central system of spurs, reached from the right above the initial rock barrier; in the summit zone it follows the gulley to the left of the spur.

Tips: There are several good possible campsites, a retreat is dangerous during a snowfall. Therefore, plenty of food should be kept in the central high camps. The storm camp — from where a summit bid is launched — is best placed immediately under the Merkl Gully. Climbing equipment should be adequate for moderate difficulties on rock and extreme difficulties on ice. The ideal time to make the ascent is in the months between May and September.

The Central buttress of the Rupal Face offers the logical route up the South Face of Nanga Parbat. The Southeast Pillar to the right is harder, and dangerous, and the Schell-Route to the left barely touches the face itself.

The History

It was around the middle of the last century that Nanga Parbat, the 8,125 m high western buttress of the Himalaya, was discovered by Europeans. The Schlagintweit brothers from Munich, who had travelled widely in India and High Asia, penetrated the Himalayas and drew a panoramic view which is the first known picture of Nanga Parbat. Shortly afterwards one of them was murdered in Kashgar — the 'Curse of Nanga Parbat' had begun.

Four years later came the first serious attempt to climb the mountain, and that Alpine-style! It sounds almost like a legend. At the end of the last century one of the best and most experienced of British mountaineers at that time, A. F. Mummery, came to Nanga Parbat to snatch at the stars. In 1895 with his compatriots, Collie and Hastings, as well as two Gurkha soldiers, he penetrated the inner Diamir Valley from the Rupal Valley and put up a tent on the edge of the glacier. Gazing across at the broad flank of the mountain, Mummery's eye was caught by a series of rock ribs (later to be named after him), which he considered offered a natural and possible line of ascent.

In fact, together with the Gurkha, Ragobir, as a porter and a local hunter, he succeeded in climbing the central spur of this great Rib. They climbed in nailed boots and with climbing irons*, but with no belay or abseil pegs and certainly no screw pegs. A tent was anchored on the second rock band and furnished with stores (Camp I at 5,400 m). Loads were ferried, bad weather blew up, they retreated in the face of storms, then reascended, food dumps were made at 6,100 m.

When Mummery with Ragobir struggled up over the sharp edge of the upper rib, a huge block broke away from the massive ice balcony above them and thundered down, threatening to carry everything with it. The two were overwhelmed by a billowing white cloud. Collie, who was watching everything from the foot of the face through a spyglass, saw the two men

* Early crampons.

disappear. Finished! But when the snow cloud cleared, he could again make out the two figures, moving upwards. They were unharmed! The rib must have acted like a dyke, deflecting the crashing, pulverising mass of ice to either side of it; they had not been carried away . . .

Completely unmoved by this event, Mummery and his Gurkha calmly climbed on, secure in the knowledge that the rock rib was the safest place to be; they followed it up to where it connected with the upper snowfield and continued till they were just below the last ice barrier.

Now Mummery stood at the gateway to the summit, and the gate was open. The rock spur continued through the mighty seracs. But at this point Ragobir fell ill. For Mummery the summit was within grasp, or so he believed, but his porter must come first. Bitterly disappointed, he first escorted his sick comrade down. He planned to try again and supposed that if he could bivouac in a temporary camp at 7,000 m in the Bazhin basin, he could reach the summit of Nanga Parbat the following day.

However, continuing snowfalls made it impossible to launch a further attempt on the Diamir flank, following the crest of the Rib, and Mummery resolved instead to go up to the Diama Col (6,200 m) in the farthest lefthand corner of the valley, with his two Gurkhas, cross it and inspect the possibilities on the Rakhiot side. He would meet Collie and Hastings there; they and the bulk of the equipment would follow the easier route round the Chilas side of the mountain over three small passes into the Rakhiot Valley. But Mummery never came. Hastings and Collie hurried back into the Diamir Valley. The British authorities requested the inhabitants of the surrounding valleys to search for Mummery, but no trace was ever found and it remains a mystery just how this meteor in the mountaineering firmament perished. Probably he was overwhelmed by an avalanche, but he certainly did not die on the Mummery Rib, as is often stated.

It was not until 1932 that another climbing party came to Nanga Parbat. A German-American expedition under the leadership of Willy Merkl reconnoitred the approach to the Rakhiot Valley and arrived at the conviction that it should be possible to climb the mountain from there. The team turned back without injury, but on the way home, the American, Rand Herron, having survived the avalanches and dangers of Nanga, fell to his death from the Cheops Pyramid in Egypt. 'The Demon of Nanga' had reached out for him, so it was said.

In 1934 Willy Merkl came back to Nanga Parbat at the head of an outstanding team. A camp was erected on the Silver Saddle. Peter Aschenbrenner and Erwin Schneider forced their way to just below the North Shoulder. As the party, perched high on the mountain, were preparing for a summit assault, the weather suddenly changed. They had to get out quickly. Aschenbrenner and Schneider, therefore, went on ahead to break the trail and leave the upper camps free for their following comrades. But the others did not follow. For several days they could be heard crying for help, but all attempts at a rescue foundered in the enormous masses of new snow. Three Sahibs (Wieland, Welzenbach, Merkl) and six Sherpa porters, died in the protracted tragedy. Wieland and Welzenbach under the Silver Saddle, Merkl on the Moor's Head — his porter, Gaylay, staying with him although he could have saved himself. Fidelity unto death. Drexel had died early on from a lung infection. Nanga Parbat became known as Germany's Destiny Peak — the highest goal and the greatest horror, at one and the same time. Would other expeditions follow?

In 1937 Dr Carlo Wien was the leader. He had a good team and they lacked nothing in the way of experience. They built Camp IV on a flat plateau at around 6,300 metres, a spot they considered to be perfectly safe, having rejected an earlier choice that seemed less secure. But in the night of 14–15 June, when practically the whole team and all their porters were collected at this camp because they intended to install Camp V the following day, an avalanche swept down in the night, passing over the camp like a giant paw, engulfing all the tents. It claimed the lives of seven Sahibs and nine porters. The campsite they had rejected earlier as being less safe, was untouched! Again it seemed that the hand of fate had struck.

Paul Bauer, head of the German Himalayan Foundation (Deutsche Himalaya-Stiftung) together with Fritz Bechtold and Dr von Kraus hurried from Munich by plane, although they could entertain no hopes of rescue. Without acclimatisation, they dug under the masses of ice for their dead friends. They were only able to recover their cameras and films, and diaries. Sahibs and Sherpas lay in their tents — no sign of the impending horror on their faces — buried under the deadly ice.

Paul Bauer, who was at that time one of the most experienced and prudent of German expedition-leaders, himself led a new expedition to Nanga the following year. He was a good climber and an adroit tactician, and on his expeditions would himself often go to the top. On Nanga that year, however, they had perhaps the worst weather conditions in living memory; incredible amounts of new snow, and constant avalanches. Hias Rebitsch and Herbert Ruths pressed on despite the storm to just below the Silver Saddle, but there the expedition gave up. The whole enterprise was overshadowed by the catastrophes of 1934 and 1937; there must be no repetition of tragedy, and Bauer had to be overly cautious. All participants got home safely, but this expedition, too, had its dramatic moments. On the Moor's head (7,000 m), they found the bodies of Willy Merkl and his porter Gaylay, who had perished there four years before. The porters were so unnerved by this experience that they could not be persuaded to go. And so the fourth German attempt on Nanga Parbat also failed, despite its exertions.

In 1939 Peter Aufschnaiter led an expedition to reconnoitre the Diamir side of the mountain. First of all they tried to climb the Mummery Rib, but felt that this route, which leads to the upper glacier terraces practically in a direct line with the main summit, was too dangerously exposed to avalanches. Similarly, they decided that to climb over the Diamir Glacier to the North Summit was indefensible on account of the avalanche risk. So they tried another rock rib, northeast of the Mummery Route. This expedition, it is true, suffered no fatalities, but the outbreak of war made it impossible for the German Sahibs to return home. The flight of Heinrich Harrer and Peter Aufschnaiter from their Indian internment camp into Tibet and their stay with the Dalai Lama became universally well-known afterwards.[*]

All six pre-war expeditions were repulsed by the mountain, despite the fact that they comprised the most experienced of leaders and the best of climbers. A grim force seemed to counter all efforts to climb this 'Naked Mountain' — no other Himalayan giant had claimed so many victims. Fourteen years passed by before the struggle for 'Diamir', 'the King of Mountains, as Nanga has also been called, was renewed.

It was not until 1953 that another German team laid siege to Nanga Parbat. This time the leader was Dr Karl M. Herrligkoffer and again, the attempt was being made on the Rakhiot Flank. It seemed as if once more the bad weather would rob them of success. It was only after a retreat had been called, that Hermann Buhl made his solo bid for the summit. From a little, iced-up tent at less than 7,000 metres, he began his attempt. It was the act of a man obsessed by an idea in the face of almost-certain defeat; a monstrous enterprise, seemingly contrary to all mountaineering logic and possibility of success. It mocked all Himalayan experience.

[*] 'Seven Years in Tibet' by H. Harrer (Rupert Hart-Davis 1953).

And yet — Buhl became the first man to stand on that hard-won summit. Purposeful and tenacious, he had succeeded where others had not even ventured. Hermann Buhl had earned his success. He had accomplished something that seemed unlikely to be surpassed.

After an attempt in 1961, a new Herrligkoffer expedition came to the West side of the mountain in 1963. They established Base Camp on the edge of the Diamir Glacier, under the Diamir Flank. They succeeded in climbing the steep wall at the head of the valley leading up to the Bazhin Notch, and they reached the summit. The route up this wall was technically quite difficult and the danger of stonefalls and avalanches constantly present.

After reaching the summit and bivouacing at over 8,000 metres, Toni Kinshofer, Anderl Mannhardt and Sigi Löw were plodding unroped down through an easy snow gully. Löw, as the last man, fell further and further behind the other two. They communicated with each other by shouting. He gave unclear answers, yet there seemed to be no danger. They were immediately above the Bazhin Basin, on a great, gently-sloping snow fan. Sigi Löw suddenly fell backwards down the 'harmless' gully, hitting his head so badly that he died of his injuries. Once more the Demon of the Naked Mountain had struck.

A reconnaissance in 1963, again under Dr Herrligkoffer, discovered two possible routes on the Rupal Face — one, the Toni-Kinshofer Route, took a line to the left of the face up to the West Saddle; the other was a Direttissima in the fall-line of the South Shoulder, the elegance and steepness of which cannot easily be rivalled in the Himalaya. A third possibility, the Southeast Spur, was also discussed.

The Central Direttissima was seriously attempted for the first time in the Winter of 1964. In 1968 a very strong team set off from Europe, the majority of whom had been on the Eiger Direttissima and indeed between them they could boast many climbing laurels. They reached the Merkl Icefield, the start of the main difficulties. This expedition, like the earlier Rupal Flank expeditions, was under the leadership of Dr Herrligkoffer, and it formed the basis for the success of the 1970 expedition.

Backed up by 75 years of experience on Nanga Parbat, but especially by the three previous expeditions, the Sigi-Löw-Memorial Expedition, with Dr Herrligkoffer as leader, and with both my brother Günther and I in the team, achieved the long-awaited success on the Rupal Flank. Other members of the expedition were: Michl Anderl, Gerhard Baur, Wolf Bitterling, Werner Haim, Alice von Hobe, Max von Kienlin, Günter Kroh, Dr Hermann Kühn, Felix Kuen, Gert Mändl, Elmar Raab, Hans Saler, Peter Scholz, Peter Vogler, Jürgen Winkler. With the support of a superlative team, the 5-man summit party advanced as far as the Merkl Gully, they key pitch of the Face.

When, on account of the weather, I set off alone to make a lightning attempt on the summit, Günther followed me of his own free will, and together we reached the top. Felix Kuen and Peter Scholz followed a day later. When this second team were climbing to the summit on 28 June, we had just spent a bivouac near the South Shoulder on our way back to Base Camp. Because my brother was so ill with the effects of the altitude. I felt compelled to continue down the easier Diamir Flank; it turned out to be a descent into despair. From that moment the expedition took a tragic turn.

In 1976 a small expedition from Graz, under Hanns Schell, reached the summit by following the left edge of the Rupal Flank and the West Ridge. They all came safely down.

Of the twelve German-speaking climbers who have reached the summit of Nanga Parbat, only six are alive today. Hermann Buhl fell to his death on Chogolisa in the Karakorum on 27 June 1957; Günther Messner, my brother, who stood with me on the summit on

Günther Messner.

27 June 1970, died two days later at the foot of the Diamir Flank, buried under an avalanche; Sigi Löw was killed eight years before whilst descending the mountain; Toni Kinshofer, who was without doubt one of the best of the German post-war climbers, died in a fall at Battert a few years after his Nanga climb; Peter Scholz died on the Aiguille Noire; Felix Kuen, who had made first ascents of four Big Walls, took his own life on 23 January 1974.

Despite these ironic chance events, it is nonsense to talk of the Curse of Nanga Parbat, and if Nanga has become Germany's 'Destiny Peak', it is not because of any demon reigning there, but simply because it is so immeasurably bigger than we mere mortals.

Odyssey on Nanga Parbat

It is seven years
since that first ascent of the Rupal Face, seven years during which I have climbed many other worthwhile peaks and won many other new experiences. It is said that a man changes every seven years, that in that time all his cells are renewed. But what about his spirit?

I am not going into detail here of those forty days my brother and I spent on the Rupal Face, days into which we put every last effort in order to reach the top of this, the world's highest rock and ice face. The retreat down the Diamir Flank that followed, which offered us our only chance of getting back to the valley alive, remains without a shadow of doubt my hardest mountaineering experience. But it doesn't belong here. It was a descent into despair, as I have said, not a climb on a Big Wall. It is enough for me today just to remember the hours that Günther and I spent on the summit together, to arouse emotions that show the whole enterprise in a dimly peaceful light.

So much has been written in the intervening years of that first ascent of the Rupal Face, of the 'Red Rocket Affair', of Nanga Parbat itself, that it is easy enough to find out the full sequence of events and to form one's own opinion of them by comparing all the versions against each other.

During the course of this expedition, I died.
Not 'died' in the true sense of the word — I don't believe in reincarnation — it wasn't my body that died, but my spirit, my will and all my hopes. Up on the Merkl Gap, I had the feeling that a part of myself was rolling away, and in the Diamir Valley afterwards, my very last hopes disappeared. And when I found myself once more, it was with a new spirit, a new will, new hopes.

When I set off for Nanga Parbat, and in all those years beforehand when I had been intensively pre-paring myself for the Rupal Face, it was the prospect of the struggle against and conquest of Nanga Parbat that concerned me, the conquest of the highest face on earth. Today, looking back, it's all the same to me, it is not so important to have been one of the first to have climbed the Rupal Face.

Yet at the time our every thought was directed towards this face. Günther and I both wanted it to be us to reach the summit, and behind this wish of course, there stood a good measure of egoism. In a letter that Günther wrote home to our parents and brothers and sisters a few days before the summit bid, this comes over clearly. Even when our chances of making this wish come true seemed very slight, we did not relinquish our ambition.

Rupal Valley, Tap-Alp, 15 June 1970

Dear Parents, dear Brothers and Sisters,

Today it is exactly a month since we arrived at the mountain. On 15 May we set up our main camp here on the Tap-Alp. And since then much has happened and altered. The snow has melted for quite a long way up the mountain and the Tap-Alp has become green. It is full of flowers, resembling a cottage garden in places. Half-wild yak herds wander around this romantic, wild, basin-shaped, high valley, and scrawny horses come up to recover from a harsh winter.

I am sitting almost exactly above Base Camp as I write this and can look down over the whole valley basin. The Alp itself is a meadow, almost as flat as the top of a table. In the middle are trees. Storms and avalanches have left their mark. Every second tree is withered and barren of leaves. Every evening our porters collect five or six of these dead trees to make a massive camp fire.

To the North, immediately above us, stands the Rupal Flank, 4,500 metres from foot to summit, unbelievably impressive. Two enormous moraines border the Alp to the west and east. To the south the Rupal Peak dominates the valley. It has never been climbed yet and it is the secret ambition of our 'amateur climbers' to reach its summit.

In the northwest corner of the Alp, our Base Camp is situated, close to two springs. They are five minutes away. Our tent village comprises 15 tents, including porters' tents, kitchen and mess tent, leader's tent. Everything is nicely

'A period of fine weather set in. We needed these days for the first, and perhaps also the last, summit bid. On the evening of the 18 June, the Messner brothers with Werner Haim, Elmar Raab and twelve high-level porters set off for Camp I . . . the next day in the early morning they reached the site of Camp II, which had been totally engulfed, and immediately set about digging it out', so begins Dr Karl M. Herrligkoffer's description of the last climb in his official expedition report 'Kampf und Sieg am Nanga Parbat' (Struggle and Conquest on Nanga Parbat).

'On the 27 June at about 06.10 hours, I saw a black dot on the icefield halfway up the Merkl Gully, which was moving upwards relatively quickly', wrote Dr Herrligkoffer. This dot was Reinhold Messner, who had set out on a lone bid for the summit. His brother Günther followed. They reached the summit in the late afternoon, then climbed down the Diamir Flank (both photos).

contained and in the centre of the circle stands a pole with the German and Pakistani flags. Everyone has his own tent where, if it rains or snows, he can retreat and write, read, sleep; somewhere where he can stow his personal belongings — and find them again. Reinhold and I are sharing a 3-man tent. We are very comfortable. We have air-mattresses and sleeping bags, of course, and nobody tells us how our own tent should be organised. That was just a glimpse of Base Camp, the mother camp to all our high camps.

Why I am writing to you today from Base Camp when the letter I wrote in Camp III has not yet gone down? For a good ten days here, all hell has been let loose; not amongst the team who work together and co-operate well, no — it's the weather that's been playing havoc. Since 3 June we have had snow storms practically without ceasing. In the high camps great quantities of new snow fall every day (a metre and more!). Avalanches thunder down the incredibly steep flanks. The only good thing to say is that Reinhold and I have selected the different campsites and taken every care that they should be protected from avalanche or stonefall danger.*

Camp I is under a big rock overhang; Camp II under a vertical serac some 20 metres high, with a ridge just above that divides the avalanche and sends them down to the left and right of the camp; Camp III is our celebrated Ice Dome, similarly protected from avalanches; we haven't yet moved into Camp IV (we reached the level for it on 3 June but had to retreat on account of snowdrifts).

With all the new snow, the face is extraordinarily treacherous right now. For as long as the avalanche danger persists, we won't be able to go on ferrying loads, even in fine weather. Over the past twelve days all the high camps have had to be evacuated and the whole team is now back in Base Camp. As I wrote in my other letter, Reinhold and I spent ten days initially at Camp III in a snowstorm, hoping for better weather; we stayed on up there as the descent became progressively riskier.

The 10 June was a better day, calmer and sunnier, and a lot of the new snow had either avalanched off or settled. During the day the other members of the team, who had been in Base Camp since 5 June, climbed up to reoccupy the camps. Everyone was in high spirits and it seemed as if we were about to see a change in the expedition's fortunes. On the 11th, Reinhold and I wanted to climb up to Camp IV again, locate a good place for it on the lower edge of the

* Günther Messner is referring here to the sites of the high camps, not to the Main (Base) Camp or the Winch Camp.

The Diamir Flank on Nanga Parbat (8,125 m). 'For our current Himalayan experience, this mighty face above the Diamir Glacier is intimidating enough' pronounced Prof. Dr G. O. Dyhrenfurth in his 'Buch vom Nanga Parbat'. Without expedition back-up, the two Messner brothers descended the 3,500 metre Diamir Face after climbing the South Face. Reinhold Messner continued alone back down the valley after his brother was buried at the foot of the face. Despite very serious frostbite injuries and total exhaustion, he forced his way on to the first inhabited settlements. A year later he embarked on his Big Wall Climbing programme.

After several bivouacs without shelter, plagued with hallucinations, thirst and hunger, Reinhold Messner reached the bottom of the valley at the foot of the Mazeno Peaks. Dr Herrligkoffer was 'filled with the deepest dismay and concern at the plight in which the Messner brothers might find themselves' (quotation from book) after he had learned from the second summit pair, Kuen and Scholz, that the Messner brothers wanted 'to take a different descent route'.

Merkl Icefield, and erect a tent. The food that we had carried up on 3 June would have lasted for another two or three days, by which time the others should have come up with fresh supplies. But in the morning we were greeted by a shower of sleet and black clouds encircling Nanga. Quickly we crawled back into the tent. At 8 o'clock all hell was let loose again. We felt pretty fed up. We would soon have spent a full two weeks at Camp III at 6,000 metres, and we felt it was now absolutely necessary that we soon move. We decided, therefore, that on the 12th, or the 13th at the latest, we would climb down if the weather was really no better. As it happened we came down on the afternoon of the 13th and, thanks to good acclimatisation, we were able to do so in a very few hours.

The weather report from Peshawar continued to be bad and the rest of the team (nine men) cleared the other high camps on 14 June (their food supplies had also nearly given out, since the high-level porters had been virtually at a stand-still since 3 June). Today, 15 June, everyone is together in Base Camp (18 Sahibs, 15 high-level porters and our 25-year old Liaison Officer). The mist hangs right down to the Tap-Alp and it drizzles most of the time. Avalanches are thundering away up on the mountain. As you can imagine, their noise is very impressive, even when you can't see anything of them. As a result of this filthy weather, hopes for the summit are getting smaller and several people are saying there isn't much sense in going on.

A few of us don't want to give up on any account and say it is cheaper to stay here longer than to come out again. If it were absolutely necessary, we could stay till 15 July, because it has often been shown that fine weather can accompany the start of the monsoon period. Unfortunately food supplies will be a bit short by then. Already we are talking about some rationing here in Base Camp. Today, for instance, we have bought a young yak (200 rupees, about 156 DM) which we can eat over the next few days. We would like to buy eggs, meal, potatoes and rice from the farmers, eating as much local food as possible here in Base Camp and saving our own precious food for the high camps. This way we can avoid a big drain on our supplies. We still

Günther Messner, overwhelmed by an avalanche on the descent.

have plenty of tins of vegetables, and rhubarb grows wild here in profusion.

Our porters and a few local farmers are just off to catch a young ox to roast on a spit. They look for all the world like Stone Age men as they chase behind the half-wild cattle.

Everyone is fine, except our youngest — Peter Vogler — who is not at all well. He was brought down in great pain from the Winch Camp. The diagnosis is pleurisy. Reinhold and I are keeping fit although we have lost weight. Our noses have peeled again.

'Reinhold with his frostbitten digits was completely exhausted and his progress through the Diamir Valley in the direction of Gilgit was only possible with the help of shepherds, farmers and an officer', described Felix Kuen in his book 'Auf den Gipfeln der Welt'.

Every four or five days the post runner comes up, an agile little farmer from Tarshing; he brings our letters and eggs. He either rides or comes by jeep and sometimes stays overnight, going back to Gilgit the next day. The roads should be mended again by now; when we arrived, they were quite useless and we had to come in on foot. Tomorrow, therefore, he will go down again with about 20 letters from us, most of which we wrote at Camp III during the bad weather.

And how is it back home? Have the schools broken up yet? We are curious to know where you will all be when we come home. Have Helmuth, Erich and Waltraud received our letters? The post is very slow and I believe that many letters have gone astray.

The ox has been slaughtered and we are celebrating by having offal and barbecued meat with plenty of vegetables.

You can write to us until the end of June because we will pick up post in Gilgit as well as in Rawalpindi, if necessary. How long the return journey will take depends on the weather. In any event it will be six days from Base Camp.

Looking forward to seeing you all again soon.

Auf wiedersehen
Günther and Reinhold

But there was to be no 'Wiedersehen',

Günther was lost after the traverse of Nanga Parbat. I came home alone — and as a different person.

In the years since then, I have had to defend myself against all the persecution and the many accusations that this Nanga Parbat traverse brought in its wake. I am well aware that it doesn't help at all to keep going back over the whys and wherefores of the accident. And I am no longer bitter about the outcome of the expedition, just unbearably sad that my brother never returned.

I have finished with the Big Disenchantment, which engulfed me completely just after the event; I have now begun to pay more attention to what I feel inside, rather than to listen to what other people believe I ought to feel, or try to persuade me. For the decision to climb down the Diamir Flank, I alone bear the responsibility. Whether it was the right decision or not, similarly, I alone can know — although there are

Reinhold Messner returned to the Diamir Valley in 1971, 1973 and 1974. The local inhabitants who in 1970 at the start of his Odyssey could only stare at him uncomprehendingly and then carry him down the valley, have in the meantime become his friends. Whether he could have made his lonely retreat if he had known beforehand of the distance and the rigours in front of him, he cannot today say.

many people who have taken it upon themselves to pass judgement on it.

The result has been that I have now taken the responsibility for my own life into my own hands, and I direct my actions less towards what other people expect — or are prepared to sanction — and much more towards what I want to do. I no longer even feel the need to rail against what is considered 'impermissible' as I did when younger.

During that expedition, and ever since then, I have

Deep inside himself, Reinhold Messner carries the indelible
impressions of the Diamir Valley: on the edge of the forest and later
on the flat mud-roofs of the stone huts, he saw, during his return
march, people moving about — men, women, children. 'They remind
me of my second birth-place, of my new childhood. Not of an
exciting time, rather a long helplessness' he says today.

directed my own experiences, and that is the only way to bring an Odyssey to an end, an Odyssey that started more than seven years ago in those fateful days after the first ascent of the Rupal Flank. It has been my good fortune to 'die' young; I have time left to busy myself with the fundamental questions of existence which the experience raised. Bizarre events like these certainly plunge a man into despair at the time, but for a young man they do carry the legacy of a deepening of his perceptions.

The Nanga-Parbat-Odyssey has given me the strength to face any future hazards squarely and accept or reject them, and every single hazardous enterprise I now undertake — whether it is 'successful' or no — is for me today an invisible ingredient of my life, of my fate.

I believe that if I accomplished the traverse of Nanga Parbat, and didn't allow the many disputes that followed, to beat me down, then there cannot be much left to fear. Yet even this belief is an illusion. To yield to it could be dangerous. So I am prepared for the next disappointment when it comes — it is part of the inevitable, dramatic threat of human existence.

'Perhaps it is a good thing, sometimes, not to be able to see any way out, to have to rely completely on oneself' says Reinhold Messner today, seven years after the 'biggest adventure of expedition history', an adventure that he miraculously survived, 'to move purely instinctively, to look around, to look forward.'

A good year after the Nanga Parbat expedition, Sergio Bigarella and Reinhold Messner set off through the New Guinea jungle to the Carstenz Mountains. During their return march they had to go without food for almost five days; notwithstanding this, they survived.

The Will to Survive

Experience shows that of the most successful mountaineers of any generation, only half die from 'natural causes'. The others plunge to, freeze to, or otherwise meet, their deaths in the mountains. Alpine history confirms this situation as a brutal reality; it used to make me think of giving up big mountaineering. Is it, then, pure chance who doesn't come back and who survives? Or is there some connection between survival and the practical experience and circumspection of a climber? Today I am convinced that one of the most decisive factors for enduring in a life-or-death situation, is the will to survive. I believe that this can even have some influence over objective dangers. I am not saying that a man's will can stop rocks breaking away or hinder the passage of avalanches — only that a man who is in contact with himself and his surroundings, is unlikely to find himself in their path. I would stick my neck out and suggest that the mentally well-adjusted climber won't perish on a mountain — or, put another way, every mountain accident has a human ingredient. And if I survived on Nanga Parbat, it was only because at the time I had an overwhelming desire to survive. For all that, I nevertheless did 'die' in a sense, and today I feel that to actually die would be easier after the experience. I am no longer afraid of the prospect of death, nor yet afraid of life. But the survival instinct I am talking about, has little to do with all that; it depends upon a person's enthusiasm for life and his peace of mind.

The Nanga Parbat expedition, with all that followed after — frostbitten feet, the loss of a brother who was at the same time my best climbing partner, the countless lawsuits — threw me mentally off balance for a time. But soon with the help of new activities and new friendships, inner calm and strength were reborn in me.

In recent years, I have become more and more preoccupied with the figure of Hermann Buhl, the first person to climb Nanga Parbat, but who, after his great

114

climbing achievement in 1953, was strongly criticised. And yet Buhl did not give up climbing. On the contrary, he went on to scale the most difficult Big Walls of his day in the Western Alps and took on new expedition goals. In 1957 he set off for Broad Peak, his second eight-thousander. At that time, Buhl was without question the most successful mountaineer in the world, yet he was a controversial figure amongst top climbers. Even former rope-partners were hostile to him. Was this because he had achieved fame outside of mountaineering circles, or something about himself? He quite obviously suffered as a result of this attitude and gradually his whole personality changed.

I am always asking myself whether Buhl's will to survive suffered in some way, whether the Hermann Buhl who walked off the cornice in thick mist in 1957, was indeed the same Hermann Buhl who struggled back alone from the summit of Nanga Parbat in 1953, completely exhausted but determined to live. How much Buhl must have suffered under the constant personal attacks, most of which came from his erstwhile closest circle of friends. Each new achievement brought him more recognition, but at the same time, more controversy. He could not avoid it. Did he then perhaps toy with the idea of surrender?

Be that as it may, finding myself in the crossfire of the critics some two decades later, I have often wished that I was buried along with Günther on the Diamir Flank. When we stood on the summit of Nanga on 27 June 1970, our will to survive was so great that we were able to find our way down the unknown Diamir side of the mountain. This was only possible because I searched out a passable route, step by step, retracing at least a thousand metres of height. I climbed back once because a serac blocked the way, again when a rock step seemed too risky for Günther, and a third time when crevasses barred all further progress. I doubt whether today I would still have the same psychological strength to get myself out of a similarly lethal situation, but I would like to win back that strength. These days I see the biggest threat to inner harmony — which I consider to be the prerequisite for all forays into 'border-line' territory — coming less from criticism and persecution than from depression, changing personal relationships and disillusionment.

I don't know whether it would be a good thing for a person if he didn't care what happened from one day to the next, I don't know if that would herald for him a period of happiness or one of stress. I only know that he would then have to give up extreme climbing if he wanted to survive; he would be a potential suicide on a Big Wall.

And I am convinced that psychological erosion presents a serious threat to the extreme climber, the constant wear and tear that is caused by sustained personal attack, disillusionment and, more than anything, by a shattered emotional life. Without noticing it, a man loses, drip by drip, his will to live, and he needs this will to face life-or-death situations. Without it, he could no longer instinctively do, or want, the right thing. Walter Bonatti resigned himself to this fact and withdrew from hard mountaineering when the many grudgers began to gnaw away at his psyche. Or was it the unconscious reaction of so experienced a man, to rescue his 'eroded' survival instinct? I don't know.

I feel I must be particularly wary on this point. There are still a few big mountains I am anxious to climb, and they are bound to present, sooner or later, some potentially-dangerous situation. Because of this, I am searching for a new balance within myself, training myself in the art of patient acceptance. It can serve no purpose to try to outwit the many jealous and critical people, to seek to punish their triviality with arrogance. My main desire is not to let them affect me at all, they must be all the same to me, just as to the Buddhist the desires of the world are all the same. That is the only way I can ensure that one day I, too, don't walk over the edge.

Dhaulagiri South Face

Dhaulagiri (8,167 metres) floats high above the sub-tropical jungle of Nepal. For a long time it was considered to be the highest mountain in the world. Now, this elegant summit — visible in fine weather from Pokhara — is known to be the sixth among the fourteen 8,000 metre peaks. The local people call it the White Mountain (dawala — white, giri — mountain).

Its Normal Route, the Northeast Ridge — first climbed in 1960 by an international expedition led by the Swiss climber, Max Eiselin, and since then repeated by American, Japanese and Italian expeditions — is recognised as being very difficult. Its South Flank, described by Professor G. O. Dyhrenfurth as 'one of the most appalling walls in the Himalaya', is the highest unclimbed mountain face in the world.

Uncannily steep, the giant wall rises a good 4,000 metres and was the objective of a small expedition that I organised and led in the Spring of 1977.

Again I joined forces with Peter Habeler, who was my partner on Hidden Peak, and for such an ambitious and formidable enterprise, we added two other internationally-known climbers: Michael Covington, a top American free-climber, and Otto Wiedemann, one of the most promising of the young German mountaineers.

But the South Face of Dhaula is more than a Big Wall. It is very secretive — and it kept its secret. Like an oracle, I stumbled today on the words of an old Ghurka soldier: 'Dhaulagiri is like five fingers on a hand. The first and last fingers are deadly, the two others too dangerous, only the central finger would present a way to the summit.'

Dhaulagiri — the White Wall overlooking the Nepalese Jungle

In its lower section, the 4,000 metre high Dhaulagiri South Face falls away precipitously. Higher up seracs are poised. Without success, Reinhold Messner (photo below) sought a safe route to the summit.

Without taking my left hand

from its hold, with my axe I could knock down the icicles that hung like a thick, tattered curtain from an overhang. The sun had come up early and now at 7.30 on a clear morning, it was already hot and dry. I wondered what it would be like at midday if it was so sultry already. The light morning breeze carried with it fine crystals of snow, and they seemed to hang poised in the air, constantly sparkling.

We were in that part of the initial gully on Dhaulagiri's South Pillar, where it narrows into a vertical throat — mixed terrain crossing an overhanging rock spur. Keeping to the right, we climbed towards a ramp that led upwards for a few hundred metres to another vertical rock buttress. Above that clung an uneasily steep icefield — we had seen it in the morning as we approached the climb, it had a gradient of 60° or more. Seen from here, it looked for all the world like a church roof rising in the sky above us.

There was not much snow

on the loose, dark rocks, so that at first we could climb without crampons. Every time I lingered on a stance with Peter belaying me, I would crane my head back as far as it would go, trying to spy out a possible way ahead. Could we get any further, or would our expedition come to an end here and now? Finding another possibility, we knew we could go a bit further at least.

No sooner had we put the short traverse to the ramp behind us, however, than once more I began to wonder whether it would not be better to turn back. The rocks rising to the left above us were not at all like rocks of an Alpine face, they were gigantic rock fragments clinging to the mountain with seemingly nothing to bind them there. I could not but wonder, standing there, why the whole lot did not crash down upon us.

Despite this constant menace, however, I was glad to be climbing the face at last. Happy to have arrived at my long-desired goal, this vertical corner of the world where no-one had been before, mysterious and alluring.

As we advanced, hold-by-hold, across this unknown territory the tensions that had preceded the expedition, melted away, although the way the face leant out so alarmingly above us, created new apprehensions. The fear of avalanches was constantly with us, but we climbed on. We wanted to know, once and for all, whether this face was possible or impossible for us. Whether it was too risky, or whether a safe route to the summit did exist.

Friability, great verticality and daily storms characterise the climbing in the Dhaulagiri South Face (pictures of the centre of the face). Moreover the constant threat of avalanches add to the danger. The Messner expedition decided to turn back. The risks attached to this face seemed too great.

Taking small steps

we traversed up towards the Ramp. Far away to our right we could see the Annapurna Group, enveloped in haze and seemingly of some different world, and way below in the valley the undulating green-black hills of the Nepalese jungle, packed tightly one behind the other in compact formation all the way to the horizon. Rising above them was the finely-detailed snow ridge and the summit of Manapati. Here and there a white cloud floated over the forested hills and if one looked closely, one could see birds flying in and out of the treetops.

Suddenly there was an eagle in the sky. I stamped a big step in the spongy snow, dug the shaft of the axe well in and held it tightly; I pointed in the direction of the circling bird. 'It's an eagle' cried Peter, who had only just seen it. He too paused, gasping for breath, 'an eagle — over the glacier!' He turned to look in the direction of the Annapurna Group.

'It's climbing higher', I shouted, 'It's coming!'

'Where!' Peter cried back.

'It's almost as high as us — between the Southeast Ridge and us.' Peter hung tightly onto the belay peg, leant backwards and bellowed up to me 'It won't find much to eat up here — it's too steep even for wall-creepers!'

'Or too dangerous', I called down. Then climbed on.

The ice

here had a gradient similar to the lower section of the Droites North Face. We came to a band of rock barring the way ahead, and above it rose another ice-shield, steeper and more threatening.

We had already reached the lower edge of the rocks when suddenly a snowslide flowed over us, giving us such a fright that we considered going back down. The resolve to give up this face and not to make another attempt, and our desire to rebuild our confidence,

were at that moment as close together as lightning and thunder. But once the evil moment had passed, the snow dust settled, and the avalanche disappeared below — it had hit a kind of prow above us which had scattered the bulk of it away from us — we again took courage. But more than that it was curiosity to see what lay ahead that took us over the next step.

Meanwhile we had reached a height of 6,150 metres above sea level. Looking left we could see the western outliers of the Dhaulagiri Group; looking the other way, to our right, was the whole Annapurna Massif.

For a good half rope's length
we ventured out over the rocks and onto the ice-shield. It was incredibly steep, as hard as anything I had ever climbed on ice. Suddenly it cracked — an avalanche! Then we knew we could go no further. Not in this weather. There was simply too much snow, it had been falling day after day. It wasn't that our enthusiasm waned, it was simply that our good sense outweighed it, our good sense in recognising that this face was impossible in these prevailing conditions without taking over-many chances.

It was not too difficult a decision, to give up.

So it was agreed
and we didn't linger too long at our highest point, for every pause spelt danger, and every minute of delay meant that the retreat over the glacier would be that much more strenuous. The snow would surely have grown very soft by now. We abseiled down, surviving a second avalanche and saw the wisdom of our decision confirmed. We congratulated ourselves on settling for the only logical solution in this situation.

I now looked at the ice slopes and broken rocks with

fresh eyes, with relief. No longer did I see them as a possible route to the summit, as I had a few hours previously. In some mysterious way, everything seemed now to have changed, even myself. And I began to feel as if I were immersed in a great lake, not in order to sink to the bottom, but to clamber out again. The sun, shining through the cloud, soothed my jangled senses, and a relieving tiredness washed over me. Putting a piton into a crack of rock made me think of flowers on a sun-warmed wall.

The clouds drew in; the crevasses on the glacier below yawned darkly. Stones rolled past us, bouncing and rebounding in great arcs, till they disappeared below. Their sound hung in the air after they had gone. Everything seemed to be in motion: the snow under our boots, the stones, the cloud in the valley. For a long time I watched a banner of cloud in the shape of a fish hanging over Annapurna; then it suddenly dissolved into the blue sky.

I would loitre longer than necessary at the belay stances and gaze at the jungle far out on the horizon, or at a patch of sky between the clouds, as if to try and keep the sensation after they were gone.

I remembered idly the press contracts we had entered into in connection with this Dhaulagiri expedition, but I didn't let them bother me, nor the thought that our food supply at our first high camp would soon give out.

As we came back into camp, Gyaltsen, one of our Sherpas, was standing in front of the tents. Over his thick pullover he wore his down jacket, and I noticed his boots were unlaced.

In the mid-day heat
it was sticky inside the tents, and we came out to lie in the fresh air. The bright snow slopes stretched out below in a blue light, glittering, soothing surfaces. The

face with its serac zones and rocky outcrops, with the glacier below and the sky above, presented a perfectly unified picture; clouds would gather and muffle it from view, then just as suddenly float away again and reveal the scene.

How easy it was

to live with defeat! Perhaps only because I had considered the possibility beforehand and come to terms with it. Throughout the preparations, failure seemed not an impossibility and I learned to accept the idea. From the beginning, as often as I thought of the summit, I thought also of a possible withdrawal before it was reached.

The sun disappeared behind a rock buttress and it became cooler. We shivered and went back inside our tent for the comfort of our insulated mattresses, our warm clothing, sleeping bags, stove and food. There wasn't much to say, we just relaxed.

After a while Peter began writing in his diary. He glanced at me over the open pages thoughtfully. I returned his gaze and each of us relived in the eyes of the other, the experiences of the day; we saw Dhaulagiri; we saw the whole expedition.

We had failed

and so there would be no reason to write more than a line or two about these few dramatic hours or about the undertaking, were this any other mountain, or were the climb on any other face.

Is it premature to talk of failures?

Just to survive on this 4,000 metre wall of rock and ice, in the drumfire of stonefalls, the thunderous frenzy of avalanches, is a very powerful feeling. To climb further would have been suicide. Right up to the point where we turned back, we were totally committed to the project. Is that, then, failure?

We had begun to study the South Face

soon after we had erected Base Camp at 4,000 metres in a very pleasant spot with little lakes and patches of green moss. It outstripped anything I had ever seen before so far as steepness, danger and wildness were concerned. Massive icefalls hung poised to fall; indeed pieces were forever breaking off and thundering to the foot of the face. It would go on for minutes at a time, the earth shivering, and the air blast with its cloud of powder snow would reach us two kilometres away from the foot of the face.

Our plan was not to climb the middle section but to attempt the left-hand rock spur, which appeared to be the only justifiable route. Because we hadn't yet put hand to rock on the face proper, we felt confident enough — if at the same time, somewhat sceptical, because it snowed day after day. By 10 o'clock each morning at the latest, it would get very gloomy and to the ice avalanches, would be added the new-snow avalanches. In the four weeks we spent at Base Camp, there were only two relatively fine days on which it did not snow.

And all the time we were fruitlessly looking for a route, a drama was playing itself out in Base Camp. Bruno Moravetz (Mora), who was in charge of the ZDF tv camera team, which was supposed to be making a documentary of the climb, fell ill from the effects of altitude. There was no possibility of a helicopter putting in whilst this bad weather continued, and so I had to send him down to the valley with the expedition doctor, Dr Berghold, and my brother, Hansi. He was on the verge of death.

As they set off down through the snowdrifts, Mora with the oxygen flasks on his back, reeling and staggering, I thought: it must have been like this when Scott with his two last comrades came staggering back from the South Pole.

The whole approach route,

when I think of it now, is like the scene of a nightmare; and Mora, exhausted as he was, had to get down again — through rivers, over the narrowest of ice bridges, through narrow ravines and mossy rainforest, through knee-deep avalanche snow and blocks of rock and ice as big as dining tables.

It had taken us almost two weeks to get from Pokhara to Base Camp; no-one had ever been through the last gorge before us.

We had not hurried. It has never been my way to be so impatient as to risk everything before reaching a Base Camp, nor to gallop hastily down after a successful climb. It's too dangerous in any case. Once we had arrived, all four of us busied ourselves with the preparations for attempting the face, win or lose. At last on the 9th April, the four of us — Peter Habeler, Otto Wiedemann, Michael Covington and I — built our first high camp at 5,350 metres, safely tucked under some rocks.

We were very pleased.

It was 1,350 metres higher

than Base Camp, which was an enormous difference. Bigger expeditions with a lot of gear and many Sherpas and oxygen apparatus, would give themselves one or more intermediate camps. But we had to be economical and were therefore quite pleased that we managed to accomplish so much height between the two camps.

On the next day we reconnoitred further, but discovered that in the middle section of the face, the rocks were broken and inhospitable. We would have to gain height on a literally vertical wall, where the layers of rock rest as loosely upon one another as the stones of a dry-stone wall. Gradually we began to feel that our chances were almost — if not totally — nil. With

Dhaulagiri South Face.

all our combined experience, we were not clever enough — though we didn't want to believe it — to find a route on this gigantic face, that gave us any hope of reaching the summit without getting killed on the way.

On an early morning in April, Peter Habeler and I suddenly decided to attack the middle section of the face. Without fixed ropes we climbed in Alpine style to get as high as possible, as I told at the beginning. In the first section there were several couloirs and rock steps to overcome, their difficulties far exceeding those met on the Eiger North Face. We passed the 6,000 metre mark and were advancing up an enormously steep ice field when the big avalanche struck. It was a loose new-snow avalanche, no ice, which was lucky for us. We had the feeling that it was curtains for us, that we should be blasted away. We were not, but our last hope of climbing the face disappeared along with the avalanche.

We were four members

on this expedition. I couldn't say we were friends, for we didn't really know each other very well. With the exception of Peter Habeler, who I have mentioned throughout this book and with whom I have shared my biggest mountain adventure, the others were just friendly acquaintances. From the start it was more of a union of purpose. We were all four enamoured of the idea of attempting this face. Why should we not try it together, and turn the idea into reality.

Otto Wiedemann, I had invited, because I recognised him to be a climber in peak condition, someone who is well-trained, knows what he wants and brings with him boundless enthusiasm, so necessary if one is to be able to climb such high mountains. Michael Covington, I had come to know in Alaska, having already read a lot about him and by him. I was fascinated by this young man who sees climbing quite

Clouds often resembled avalanches, and avalanches, clouds. Consequences were much the same either way: collapsed, snow-laden tents (Picture page 132).

differently from most European climbers, more casually perhaps and with less of an accent on 'goal'. I was impressed how relaxed and happy he appeared after an ascent of Mt. McKinley.

We were, therefore, a team of four climbers and of four nationalities, and each was in the top league. We didn't know each other well enough at the start to talk the usual 'kitsch' about friendship and 'all for one, one for all'. We had come together for a shared undertaking that would demand total commitment from each of us; it would also test each of us to his emotional limit. Despite this, I was certain that we would have no real differences of opinion — not if we were all after the same thing, and each was free to express his opinion. What I didn't realise until it was too late, was that language difficulties would create problems of understanding between Otto and Michael. There was nothing I could do to prevent it. A small lesson for international groups this — everyone must have a common basic language even if he is not fluent in it. But despite this communication problem, we got on fairly well.

In all our reconnaissances and attempts, none of us ever thought: 'We'll never do that!' nor 'We must do it, we are of the best and it is expected of us'. What was expected of us was that we should pull together as a team, we relied on our own judgement and in the end recognised what was right for us. We didn't allow ourselves to be influenced by all those people, spurred on by the Press, who were waiting for a summit success.

We tried, and that was all we set out to do.

There is no such thing

as a single, unswerving goal. What does exist are many possibilities which you have to discover for yourself, one of which leads on past impossibility. The longer I spent working on this face, the more slender became my connection with it. When I had begun to plan the climb, how I lingered over every detail — and towards the end I no longer stopped to consider it. When I knew all I wanted to know, when the face had finally triumphed, I did the only possible thing — I organised the return march.

Seen like that, and only like that, an expedition takes on a deeper meaning. It procures freedom.

As far as mankind is concerned,

it is completely immaterial whether the Dhaulagiri South Face gets climbed or not; it's equally unimportant if a man stands on the summit of Everest or not. The only thing that counts is the experience, the sensation the climb engenders, and that only for the person who climbed it.

On Dhaulagiri, we made our own decisions, alone; we identified with this face, fully and completely, and beyond that, we hearkened to no-one else. Where would we have been if we had paid attention to other people? Some had talked of suicide, others of self-sacrifice; there were some people who called our project one of the insanities of the twentieth century, others as the last act of heroism. But our only thought was of the face itself, and the more we came to terms with it and grappled with the task of finding an acceptable route, the greater was the fun of the climb itself, and the less important the actual success.

Having to turn back did not upset me. I was just as happy as I had been at the start. Indeed, I was no less contented than after our success on Hidden Peak two years before.

Before the first porters came up from the valley, we evacuated the high camp. And as we began the return march, I was suddenly possessed with a feeling of joy when I thought of the past few weeks, and a deep

peace at the prospect of the days ahead. As I went along, I felt that this retreat was as irrevocable as a natural law. I did not need to console myself with the hope of another attempt sometime in the future. I knew in my mind that Dhaulagiri South Face would keep its secret from me, even if there were no other ambitions left to me. For me, it would be forever unattainable. This feeling elbowed all thoughts of possible future success into the background.

We had done everything in our power, and it hadn't been enough.

And we were happy

just to have remained alive. We had now been trekking back through the valleys and over the hills of Nepal for one short week. I didn't feel a beaten man, I was as much at peace as after a successful expedition to an eight-thousander. I felt strong in myself, but no more so than anyone else; free, but no more so than anyone else. I was astonished at myself. To have such an uncanny sense of peace, simply to be walking along, nothing in front of me, nothing behind. I spoke with no-one on the way only with myself perhaps, with my surroundings, with trees, with the path, with the stream that burbled close by. And all the time I knew that the Dhaulagiri face was still at my back. When I looked around and saw it in the far distance, I could begin to appreciate just how big it was, especially that section we had not been able to climb. From below, from the spot where we turned back, it had looked short, steep, overhanging, not so huge, risky but just possibly feasible. But now, without the foreshortening effect, it stretched into seeming endlessness, into impossibility.

From a vantage point just past Chang, I turned to take a last look back, gazing at the face as if for the first time. I had been lucky. I had followed my own counsel at the start and at the finish — and I still lived.

I love these Big Walls,

I love the game of wits and nerve played in finding a way up them. But I don't love the danger. I have quite a different motive. Clinging up there, facing a desperate situation perhaps, one realises one's strength, one's potential, and one can differentiate for oneself the hairline distinction between suicide and foregoing one's attempt. To decide by one's own judgement the moment to retreat — that is a satisfying feeling, too.

So, although it may be hard for outsiders to credit, the day we decided to turn back, we were as pleased as if we had successfully reached the summit. They can gauge only by success or failure, and don't know how close the experience value is between the one and the other.

A normal route

which is a known quantity, even one that has, maybe, only been trodden by one expedition, holds no interest for me. A frustrated attempt on a virgin face of an eight-thousander, means more to me than accomplishing an ascent of a known route. With all the technical contrivances known to man, it may perhaps be possible to climb even the Dhaulagiri South Face. But I would not want to do it that way. That is why we failed, and why it was sufficient reward to have simply made the attempt, to accomplish all that we did accomplish. Reward enough to have been high, away from the everyday world, to have had time in one's own possession.

After the expedition had failed, the abseil down to the foot of the face. For the expedition there was not just one mountain, one face, one goal. Otto Wiedemann and Reinhold Messner, together with the British cameramen Leo Dickinson and Eric Jones, succeeded in climbing a six-thousander in the days that followed.

After the withdrawal of the Dhaulagiri expedition, Reinhold Messner made a reconnaissance flight over the Himalaya. For him, it opened up not only new visual, but also spiritual, points of view.

The Impossible

'We came back to Makalu Base Camp to settle our outstanding account for 1972', wrote Ales Kunaver at the beginning of his report on the successful Yugoslav Makalu South Face Expedition of Autumn 1975.

For a Big Wall Climber to assume this attitude is not without danger; it is very easy to fall into the vicious circle of the victory-at-all-costs syndrome. I have never returned a second time to any of the eight-thousander walls that have defeated me. This is not to say that I consider these walls unclimbable, necessarily — indeed the Makalu South Face from which we retreated in 1974, was climbed the following year — it is just that they don't excite me in the same way as faces I have never visited.

I have freely to admit that I place no rein on my fantasies; other people may dismiss something as impossible, but I will only acknowledge it to be so when the mountain itself spells it out in black and white. My climbing, therefore, has always been governed by my own yardsticks, and by the conditions prevailing whenever I made my tours and expeditions.

To submit to other people's guidelines and limitations has never been acceptable to me; I would far prefer to live a few short decades doing what I enjoyed, than to spend a long life conforming to rules, hedged in by convention and mediocrity. But my kind of life demands a preparedness to accept the principle of risk, as well as the ability to recognise the impossible when it faces me — the impossible, that is, for me.

This outlook helps me not to become too presumptuous, and confronted with defeat, not to despair. Someone who, after every success, has immediately to chase after another, becomes driven by an anxiety that propels him on to ever more difficult objectives, until inevitably the day comes when he can no longer keep up the pace. He is forced to retire, broken, from the field.

Ever since I was young, my climbing fortunes have gone alternately up and down and from this diversity of experience has grown in me a concern for detail, a blossoming of my fantasies and a deepening of my feelings. The sensation on that return march from Dhaulagiri, of wanting life to go on unchanged for ever and ever, brought an inner harmony not unlike the liberating moments of timelessness on the summit of Hidden Peak. Anything that can lead to this feeling of blissful release from tension after a harrowing climb is more important than the Summit or the Big Wall itself. But to give it a chance to happen, everyone has sometime, somewhere, to accept his own limitation of 'the impossible'.

'The Dragon must not die', I had written as a 20-year old in the recognition that 'the impossible' holds an everlasting fascination for the innovative climber. Today I would phrase it differently: 'Only the unknown can be overcome' — most of all, the unknown within ourselves. I have proof positive of 'the impossible', but none of the inconceivable. With this outlook I have not only survived, survived such nightmares of extreme isolation as are experienced by space travellers in science fiction, and on earth, exist almost solely in the Death Zone of the Himalayas, above the 7,500 metre frontier, up where no radio and no signal can summon a rescue helicopter; I have not only survived, I have managed to achieve a measure of what others have considered 'impossible'.

New Horizons

In this book, I have written of the Big Walls of the Alps, the Andes and the Himalaya, and the impression could be drawn that I am endeavouring to establish a framework of standards. I don't want to set any ultimate values, only new ones. My own main objective is to enlarge my comprehension of the Big Walls.

And in the same way as I have not relied on any one else's guidelines, I hope that the young climbing generation won't be content to hold to mine. Nothing of what climbers have achieved up till now, could ever have happened if at some time, some individual had not dreamed a dream, undreamt before; if someone had not, on the strength of his dream, attempted something that had never been attempted before. This

strength can only be realised if one is open to new horizons.

Following our Dhaulagiri South Face Expedition, I flew in a little Pilatus-Porter plane high over the summits of the Himalaya, and this opened new horizons for me at that time. I recorded my thoughts and impressions on tape during the flight, and I reproduce them here:

'We are now flying at about 6,000 metres in the direction of Everest. Far away in front we can already recognise the massive face of Lhotse and, behind it, the dark pyramid of the summit wall of Everest. To the right is the perfectly-shaped triangle of Makalu, and far in the background to the left, sadly shrouded in mist and cloud, that must be 'Kantsch'. Four eight-thousanders in a single view, compressed into quite a narrow space.

We are turning off now to the left, flying over the Nuptse-Lhotse Ridge with the Western Cwm, that gigantic glacier basin between Lhotse and Everest, lying below us. A sprinkling of red dots indicate the high camps of the Lhotse and Everest Expeditions.'*

Then my gaze is drawn to the black South Face of Everest. There is no snow on this face, it seems all to have blown away out of its great concavity. Incredibly steep and difficult, from this angle the face looks completely unassailable; I think with respect of Chris Bonington's expedition that succeeded in climbing it for the first time in the Autumn of 1975. Even the South Ridge, generally known as the Ordinary Route, the ridge linking the South Col with the summit, does not look simple. It is extremely long, the crest sharp in places, blunt elsewhere, and under new snow it must be fearfully exhausting to reach the summit by this route.

As we climb higher, making two small turns, the pyramid of Makalu comes into my field of vision again, and I think of the American expedition that has been trying for weeks, fruitlessly, to climb its West Face.

The team have got as high as they can go, and it is certain that during this Spring of 1977, not a single Big Wall will be climbed in Nepal. Apart from ourselves and the Americans, there have been no other attempts on the big faces. A sign that they still command the greatest respect — but that they will be the pressing tasks for extreme climbers in the forthcoming seasons.

Big Walls have fascinated me since boyhood, and although three of them have so far beaten me — the Lhotse Face, Makalu South Face and Dhaulagiri South Face — my fascination does not wane. A normal route, a known route, where maybe Sherpas select the camp sites and point out the way ahead, this does not interest me at all. Routes like this cannot give me what I seek from climbing — my own measure, the fundamental essence of myself.

I am still flying without oxygen and we have by now reached a height of more than 9,000 metres. The summit of Everest is directly below us — rock and snow in sharp contrast, exquisitely detailed, its final tip surprisingly small. I can easily imagine a man down there, like me without oxygen, but with the time and the eyesight and above all, the peace of mind, to observe the fantastic, bizarre landscape spread out around him. He would see much what I am seeing from the plane, but how much more beautiful, how much richer the experience, after he had reached the summit of Everest by his own strength, his own purpose, his own skill. How fine then to sit on top of the world and gaze all around.

Seen from the plane, the angles of these great walls appear to vary minute by minute. As the aircraft banks or with every slight movement, a face will seem to ease or steepen. One moment Everest will look

---

* In the pre-monsoon period of 1977, a New Zealand Expedition attempted Everest without Sherpa support; a German team were on the Ordinary Route of Lhotse. The New Zealanders were unsuccessful, but the Germans reached their summit — with eleven men, no less!

smaller than Lhotse, then it all changes again; another time the Everest Face seems as vertical as the North Face of the Cima Grande, but then it sinks back again and my hopes and dreams revive — hopes that this face could possibly be climbed by two people in Alpine style.

Meanwhile we have turned around; the flight is nearing its end and we are now heading towards the northwest. A glance back reveals the north side of Everest, the Chinese — or more properly, the Tibetan, side — not so steep as the south side but equally massive.

And now we are quite close to Cho Oyu, its summit like a great iced cake. To the left plunges the Southwest Face with its many gullies and ice fields — climbable possibly, but not without its dangers; to the right, the Southern Spur that curves upwards from right to left and involves mainly ice climbing; to the right of that again, a somewhat easier flank, mainly of snow and ice, but also certainly carrying a strong avalanche risk.

In the same way as for a full five years I toyed with the idea of climbing Dhaulagiri South Face, so now I conjure with the idea of Cho Oyu's South Face; perhaps that too has been in my mind for years. But this great pillar will have to wait a few more years yet because the Nepalese are not granting permits for Cho Oyu for the time being, and so long as there are no permits, no-one can visit the pillar.

A large proportion of the summits which are spread out around and beneath us, are as yet unclimbed. But it is the faces of the eight-thousanders that excite me more, even though an expedition to one of these carries only a slim prospect of success. Far more than any one of these summits — summits still to be conquered, summits upon which no man has ever trodden — I am scouring the scene below as if it must contain one valley, one flank for me. Suddenly a peak emerges, the form of which pleases me, and now I have eyes only for that one. It impresses me, I don't know its name but

I know I would like to climb it, or at least to visit it.

For me, all these mountains belong to the world, as I belong to the world, and the deserts and the rivers, the flowers and the trees. Mountains are not evil and not good, neither fiends nor friends; they simply are. And although there can be storms and avalanches on them, the mountains are not, to my mind, malevolent.

Harmony and co-existence can only be experienced in climbing if one accepts the storms, avalanches and all the other dangers as readily as one does the beauty and the perfection of shape (nowhere as rich and varied as in the Himalaya). Naturally, with the help of intelligence, one can counter the dangers and maybe possibly eliminate them, but only he who has the ability to feel at one with the high mountains and their surroundings, will continue to climb them.

This same fascination that radiates from holy mountains, especially the unclimbed ones, also surrounds unconquered faces. For me even more because I am an extreme climber and extreme climbing interests me more than anything else. I find a climb challenging only when impossibility, so to speak, hangs in the air from the outset. Inasmuch as today, with the use of every conceivable technical aid, any wall is climbable and basically nothing is impossible any more, so each untrodden, unknown face loses something of the fascination that hitherto made it an interesting climbing proposition.

Big climbing calls as much for imagination as it does for spirit and endurance, willpower and enthusiasm. Only the climber who, confronted with a particular climb, prepares a particular plan, only he who can work out an idea — can make the idea work out. The eventual outcome depends on how the idea was put into practice and how the climb developed in relation to it.

The most important thing to have resulted from all my climbing exploits, was not the summits, not the successes, nor the approbation, the most important thing at the end of the day was the awareness these climbs have given me of myself. There is always something new to learn, something to put me in a new relationship with my environment, to see the world anew.

Mountain climbing will continue to exert a fascination so long as there remain unclimbed mountains, undisturbed mountain flanks and faces. It will continue to be interesting even after everything has been 'done', but only to those open to authentic new experiences and perceptions.

After this round-flight I am sure that there are sufficient unclimbed faces to last for generations of mountain climbers, perhaps for the duration of all human time, for I saw literally thousands of them. The Diretissima on the Lhotse South Face, the South Face of Dhaulagiri, or the Southern Pillar of K2 are challenges that will long attract, will stimulate climbing thought for years ahead, projects to dream about, imagine and plan for. And between the imagined ideal that a climber constructs, between the plan and its execution, lies a portion of lifetime in which one's every sense is stretched. The word 'adventure' has been so over-used, it now signifies such a threadbare concept, that I hesitate to use it. What I am trying to say is that the quality of life in the span between the fantasy and the accomplishment, the period of proving whether a summit or face is possible or not, is greater than if mountains were not there and there were no possibilities for such fantasies and such climbs.

And in the same way as our whole life is subject to a natural rhythm, so it is with climbing — there is a progression between each single tour leading one on towards a projected goal or towards oneself — whoever seeks to skip a stage will throw himself off balance and distrub this natural flow.

So an idea precedes any climb, and success and failure alternate as do progress and retreat, expectation and disillusion. Seen thus, every rebuttal is a necessary constituent of success, a window to a new horizon.

After a success on an important summit, when one is right on the top, one can only go down. And when one is right down, one can only climb upwards again. This see-saw eventually leads to real liberation.

Everyone is free to nurture his own fantasies, everyone is unique in his own make-up, and everyone can discover for himself his own horizons. Other people's discoveries are of no real value in climbing, only one's own. Anyone who engages in top-flight climbing must be prepared for the same people who rejoice with him after a 'success' to castigate him after a 'defeat'.

Someone who is fulfilling his own ambitions does not need to listen to other people — he must be willing to accept the risk that is everpresent when one converts dreams to reality, and he must be prepared to give each one of his dreams the chance to succeed. If he follows anyone else's standards, he won't discover new horizons. What matters is to evolve one's own standards, not to allow oneself to be coerced by any outside attitudes, and above all, to find one's own goal within oneself.'

Man on the Big Wall

Big Walls remain intrinsically unimportant so long as they are approached within the context of Conquest or Defeat. Unless one visits them without preconceived notions of experience, without having learned by rote what one is expected to feel when setting out, or on the summit — then nothing will change. 'Success' will continue to be the illusory symbol of life, 'Defeat' will remain disillusion.

My wife left me during one of my expeditions, and I, in my loneliness and despair, resolved during the return march to give up Big Wall climbing. At that moment I suddenly felt as if the pillars of my earlier mountain achievements had been smashed to pieces, and I was left only with the impression that my expedition years had left behind. But it was the recollection of those moods and events that made up my experiences that finally restored my confidence.

In those days of 'Black Loneliness', it came to me that it had not been the constant spur of new successes that had kept me climbing, but that life in high places was an end in itself. I thought of the soothing 'White Loneliness' of the Big Walls, and I didn't just find consolation, I found a door to freedom. 'White Loneliness' has the power of overcoming 'Black Loneliness'. And so, there and then, I resolved once more to take up what I had just renounced.

First published in Great Britain by
Kaye & Ward Ltd
21 New Street, London EC2M 4NT
1978

First published in USA by
Oxford University Press Inc.
200 Madison Avenue, New York, N.Y. 10016
1978

Copyright © BLV Verlagsgesellschaft MbH, Munich,
1977
English translation Copyright © Kaye & Ward Ltd, 1978

ISBN 0 7182 1191 X (Great Britain)
ISBN 0-19-520062-4 (USA)
Library of Congress Catalog Card No. 78-53451

Set in Monophoto Univers by Computer Photoset Ltd, Birmingham
Printed in Great Britain by Cox & Wyman Ltd,
London, Fakenham and Reading

Photographs

Front cover: Reinhold Messner on the Hinterstoisser Traverse of the
   Eiger North Face (P. Habeler)
Pages 2–3: The Trango Tower in the Karakorum (G. Rowell).
R. Arnold (pp. 26/27, 34), Deutsches Institut für Auslandsforschung/
J. Winkler (p. 97), H. Frass (p. 16), P. Habeler (pp. 33, 35, 57),
R. Löbl (pp. 12–13), H. Muller-Brunke (p. 53), W. Nairz (p. 25),
W. Neumüller (pp. 105, 108, 112, 117), E. Pertl (pp. 38/39, 50/51,
71), V. Sella (pp. 14–15, 89, 92–93), J. Winkler (pp. 10, 19, 29,
41): all other photographs by Reinhold Messner.
Drawings: H. Hoffman (endpapers, pp. 8, 28, 40, 52, 64, 96).
E. Weinrather (pp. 4–5).

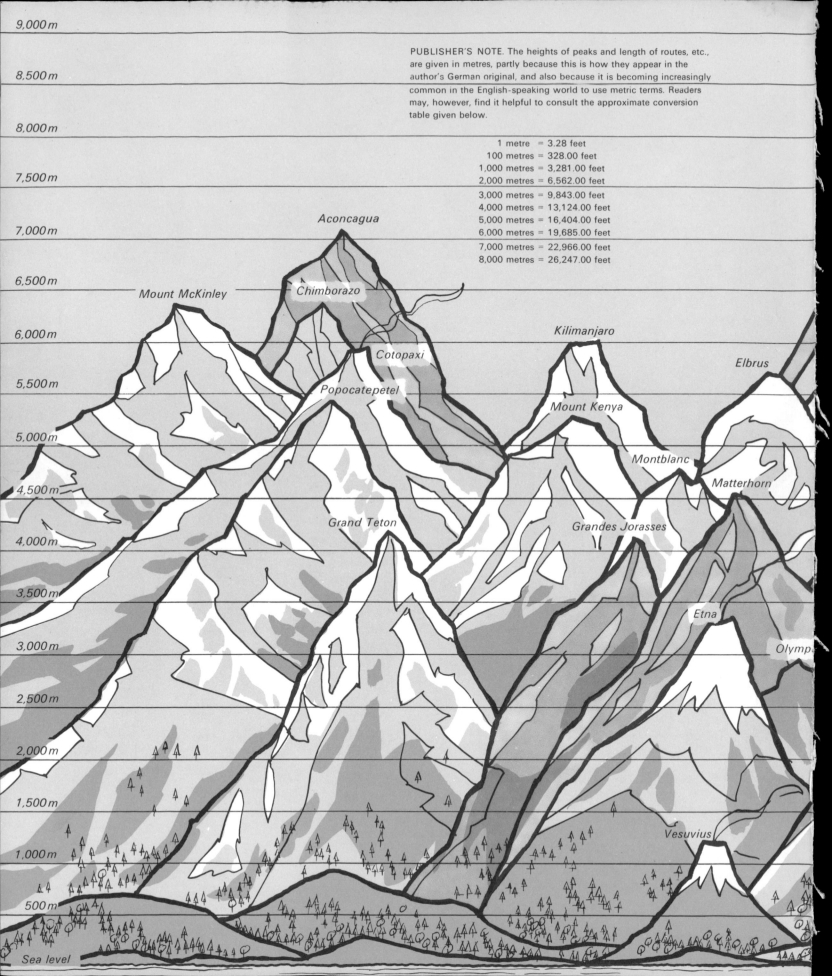

9,000 m

8,500 m

8,000 m

7,500 m

7,000 m

6,500 m

6,000 m

5,500 m

5,000 m

4,500 m

4,000 m

3,500 m

3,000 m

2,500 m

2,000 m

1,500 m

1,000 m

500 m

Sea level

PUBLISHER'S NOTE. The heights of peaks and length of routes, etc., are given in metres, partly because this is how they appear in the author's German original, and also because it is becoming increasingly common in the English-speaking world to use metric terms. Readers may, however, find it helpful to consult the approximate conversion table given below.

1 metre	= 3.28 feet
100 metres	= 328.00 feet
1,000 metres	= 3,281.00 feet
2,000 metres	= 6,562.00 feet
3,000 metres	= 9,843.00 feet
4,000 metres	= 13,124.00 feet
5,000 metres	= 16,404.00 feet
6,000 metres	= 19,685.00 feet
7,000 metres	= 22,966.00 feet
8,000 metres	= 26,247.00 feet

Aconcagua

Mount McKinley

Chimborazo

Kilimanjaro

Elbrus

Cotopaxi

Popocatepetel

Mount Kenya

Montblanc

Matterhorn

Grand Teton

Grandes Jorasses

Etna

Olymp

Vesuvius